THE TROY STETINA® SERIES

METAL LEAD GUITAR

VOLUME ONE

To access audio visit: **www.halleonard.com/mylibrary**

"Enter Code"
3570-0244-9279-1811

Cover guitar courtesy of Cascio Music

ISBN 978-0-7935-0960-7

HAL•LEONARD®
CORPORATION
7777 W. BLUEMOUND RD. P.O. BOX 13819 MILWAUKEE, WI 53213

www.troystetina.com

Visit Hal Leonard Online at **www.halleonard.com**

ABOUT THE AUTHOR

Photo Credit: Brian Beckwith

Troy Stetina is an internationally recognized guitarist, solo artist, and music educator. Specializing in rock, metal, shred, and classical-electric guitar, he has authored more than 40 book/audio and DVD methods that have guided a generation of players toward excellence and guitar mastery. Troy endorses PRS guitars, the Dimis Troy Stetina Custom Signature guitar, Engl amps, Lampifier microphones, and Dunlop strings.

Visit Troy online at www.troystetina.com for lessons, tips, videos, tour and masterclass event dates as well as current product information and full bibliography/discography.

Music CDs:
Second Soul *Beyond the Infinite*
Dimension X *Implications of a Genetic Defense*
Troy Stetina *Exottica*

Highlighted Guitar Instructional Products:
Speed Mechanics for Lead Guitar (book/audio)
Fretboard Mastery (book/audio)
Troy Stetina: The Sound and the Story (DVD)
Total Rock Guitar (book/audio)
Metal Rhythm Guitar Vols. 1 and 2 (book/audio)
Metal Lead Guitar Primer (book/audio)
Metal Lead Guitar Vols. 1 and 2 (book/audio)
Thrash Guitar Method (book/audio)
The Ultimate Scale Book (pocket guide)
Barre Chords – The Ultimate Method and Resource Guide (pocket guide)
200 Rock Licks – Guitar Goldmine Series (DVD)
Hard Rock Signature Licks (DVD)
Best of Rage Against the Machine Signature Licks (book/audio)
The Very Best of Ozzy Osbourne Signature Licks (book/audio)
Best of the Foo Fighters Signature Licks (book/audio)
Deep Purple - Greatest Hits Signature Licks (book/audio)
The Best of Dream Theater Signature Licks (book/audio)
The Best of Black Sabbath Signature Licks (book/audio)
The Best of Black Sabbath Signature Licks (DVD)

CONTENTS

WELCOME TO THE "TROY STETINA SERIES"

The "Troy Stetina Series" is a complete learning system for mastering metal and building solid musicianship. It is written by someone who specializes in metal—who plays it, lives it and breathes it, as well as teaches it—so the result is a genuine and direct approach, giving you the information and technique that you need to get playing quickly and correctly.

Taken together, the methods of this series cover the full spectrum of guitar playing, from the very beginning up to the most advanced rhythm and lead concepts, fretboard pyrotechniques, theory, how to develop your own personal lead style, and more. And it even goes beyond guitar playing with a guide to metal songwriting to help you develop that vital skill. In short, this series is designed to take you to a professional level of playing.

Brief descriptions of each of the books and videos of the "Troy Stetina Series" appear at the end of this book. Use this to help you navigate through the series, selecting what is best for you. Also, keep in mind that it is generally best to use two or three complementary books at a time, in order to have plenty of variety in your practice routine. Each book's accompanying audio enables you to use them effectively by yourself as well as under the guidance of a teacher.

FOREWORD

The Metal Lead Guitar Method is designed to bring you to top notch lead guitar playing. This book, Volume 1, is most appropriate for intermediate level players who have already been playing guitar for a year or more. Beginners are directed to Metal Lead Guitar Primer. Keep in mind that the pace of this method is somewhat ambitious, challenging you with a realistically professional level by the end of Volume 2, so take your time with it. It'll be worthwhile!

Volume 1 kicks off with a brief overview of the fundamentals in the first chapter, then launches into the first of six solos with full backing band. As the method progresses, these solos build in speed and level of difficulty. Specific highlights of Volume 1 include using various minor pentatonic, blues, dorian, and natural minor scale forms in licks and solos, a variety of articulations including different types of string bending, vibrato, palm-muting, staccato, etc., phrasing and rhythmic concepts, building a solid alternate picking format, a series of speed exercises, basic scale theory, sequencing and contouring scales, right-handed tapping, harmonics, and using the vibrato bar.

By narrowing your focus to just the skills that you need, you'll master them more quickly. And that's how this method is designed to teach metal guitar—the fastest way possible, by tackling just what a guitarist must master in order to be successful in this style. In part, it accomplishes this through a simple tab-staff notational system which eliminates the need for learning standard musical notation by applying rhythm symbols directly to the tablature numbers. Also, grid diagrams complete the shape-oriented approach and speed the learning process. Of course, learning to read standard notation is a useful skill and I highly recommend that anyone interested should pursue it, but it is arguably unnecessary here. In the end, all that matters is the sound and attitude that comes through your speaker cabinet. That is where your attention should be, and that's what this method is all about.

Good luck, and enjoy the method!

1 **This symbol indicates the audio track
number for the music examples.**

INTRODUCTION
How to Read Music in this Book

This book uses a proven tab-staff notational system which completely omits standard musical notation and speeds up the learning process for this shape-intensive playing style. If you can already read standard notation, you'll catch on to this tab-staff system in a flash. And if you don't read music, you'll find this system amazingly quick and easy to learn.

First, we'll cover the basic tablature system. Tablature, or TAB for short, is a common guitar notation system which identifies notes, or pitches, by giving the string and fret number which is to be played.

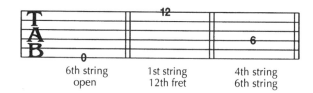

| 6th string | 1st string | 4th string |
| open | 12th fret | 6th string |

Left hand fingerings appear underneath the tablature. The fingers of the left hand are numbered as follows:

index finger — 1
middle finger — 2
ring finger — 3
little finger — 4

Indications for downstrokes and upstrokes of the pick appear above the tablature. The symbol for a downstroke is ⊓. The symbol for an upstroke is V. Other symbols will be explained as they are introduced.

Also, neck diagrams like the one below are used to show shapes and patterns graphically on the fretboard. The pattern is laid out just as if you were looking down at your own guitar fretboard. The headstock and tuning machines would be off on the left, the body of the guitar would be to the right. The short vertical lines represent the frets, the long horizontal lines represent the strings with the high "E" on top, down to the low "E" on the bottom. Notice how the pattern of dots with their associated fret numbers corresponds to the dots on the fretboard of your guitar.

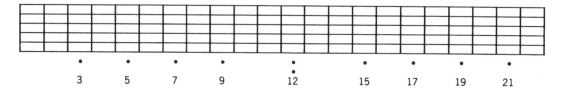

To help you read tab more quickly, particularly up higher on the neck, it is useful to memorize the fret numbers associated with the dots on the neck, above. That way, for example, you can find the 18th fret in a flash—you know that the 2nd dot above the double dots is 17, so you'll find the 18th one fret higher.

Timing and Rhythm Notation ❸

To indicate the timing aspect of the notes, we will borrow the notational symbols from standard musical notation and apply them to our tablature "notes," or fret numbers.

Whole notes and rests
are four beats each:

Half notes and rests
are two beats each:

Quarter notes and rests
are one beat each:

Eighth notes and rests
are one-half beat each:

Sixteenth notes and rests
are one-quarter beat each:

Before beginning Chapter 1, you should be able to play the following rhythm examples, tapping out the beat steadily and evenly with your foot. If you have trouble playing them or do not fully understand them, it would be helpful to refer to Metal Rhythm Guitar Volume 1 for more practice before you go on.

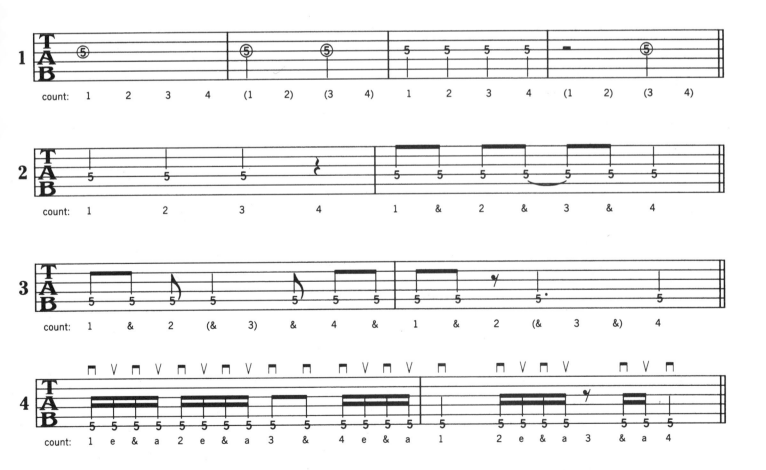

CHAPTER 1
THE MINOR PENTATONIC SCALE

The *minor pentatonic scale* it undoubtedly the most common scale in rock and metal lead guitar. It figures prominently in the lead styles of virtually all rock and metal players, from Eddie Van Halen to Kirk Hammet of Metallica, and from Jimi Hendrix to Slash of Guns N' Roses. Its applications are never-ending.

Below, it is shown in the key of A. Notice how the A5 power chord shape occupies the same position and is found within the notes of the scale pattern. The lowest note of the scale pattern, an "A" note, is the root of both the scale and the A power chord.

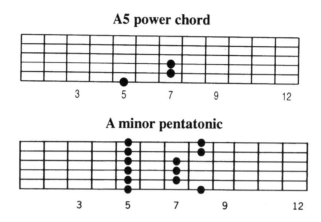

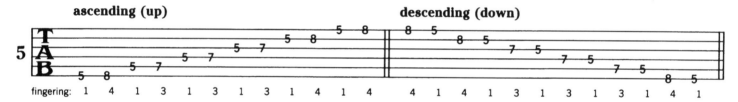

The following licks use this scale. First listen to the audio to get a feel for how they sound. Then learn the notes and see the pattern each lick makes on the fretboard. After you have them memorized, tap your foot with the underlying beat to get a feel for the rhythm. It should be steady and even.

TIP: The asterisk (*) marks the spots where you need to move from one string to another, using the same finger to fret each note. Play the first note on your fingertip, then roll your finger off one string and onto the next. This way you can change between strings without any pause or break between the sounding of the notes.

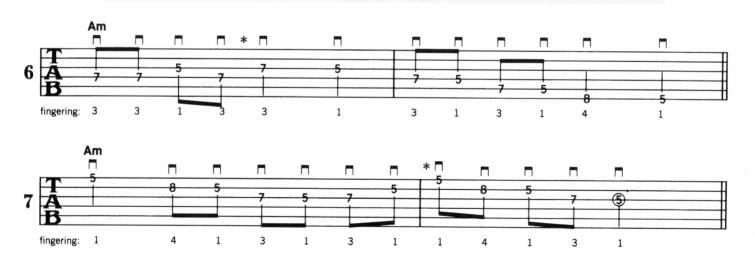

8

THE HAMMER-ON AND PULL-OFF ◆5

Play the 5th fret, third string with your index finger. Then, hammer your ring finger down on the 7th fret without picking. An "H" with a ⌒ or ⌣ indicates a *hammer-on.*

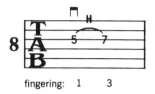

A pull-off is the opposite of a hammer-on. Place your ring finger on the 7th fret, and your index finger on the 5th fret. Pick the string, then pull your ring finger down and off the string to sound the 5th fret. A "P" with a ⌒ or ⌣ indicates a *pull-off.*

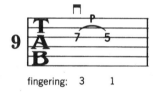

Don't confuse hammer-ons and pull-offs with ties. All use a similar symbol but ties connect only notes of the same pitch, and of course do not use an "H" or "P" symbol.

Practice hammer-ons and pull-offs in the short riffs below.

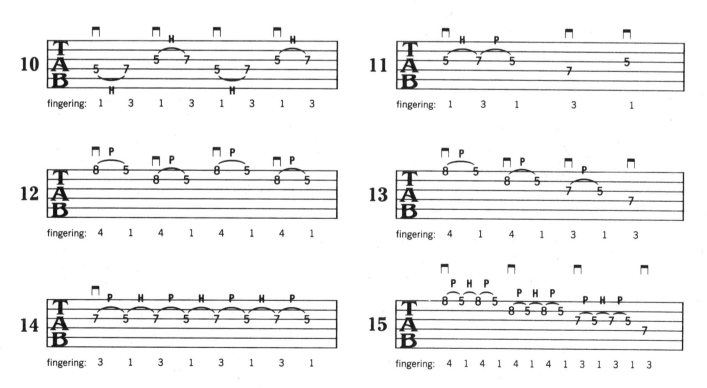

9

THE TWO-FRET BEND ◆ 6

String bending is an important part of lead playing, whereby the pitches of notes are raised to reach a target pitch. The bends here are all *two-fret bends*, so-called because the pitch of the note is raised the equivalent of two frets. They are also called whole-step or full-step bends. In the minor pentatonic pattern, the most commonly bent notes are:

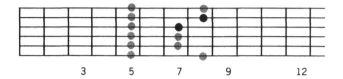

A bend is indicated by an arrow up, followed by a target pitch in parenthesis. Keep in mind that the target pitch is the fret that would have to be played on the unbent string to give the same pitch. So you do not actually play the target fret—you bend to that pitch. The following bend, for example, takes place entirely at the 7th fret:

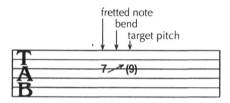

Playing two strings together while bending, known as a *double-stop bend*, is a common lead technique that we can use to get a feel for exactly how far to push the strings. For the following double-stop bend, strike both strings together, push the third string up and listen. When your bend reaches its target pitch, the turbulence between the notes will stop and both strings will sound the same because the 9th fret, third string, is the same pitch as the 5th fret, second string.

> TIP: Use your second finger right behind yor third finger, as in the the below, to reinforce the bend and give you more strength and control.

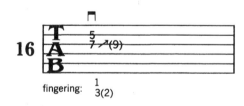

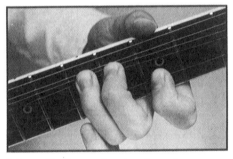

The next double-stop bend is a bit more difficult because of the added stretch. Again, when your bend is accurate, the turbulence will stop and the notes will sound the same because the 10th fret, second string, is the same pitch as the 5th fret, first string.

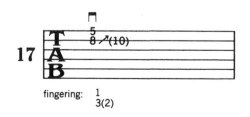

A *release* is the opposite of a bend. After a note is bent, it is released by returning it to the original pitch. The release is shown by an arrow down.

> TIP: Don't lift up pressure off of the fretboard when you release a bend, but rather, pull the string back to its unbent position, maintaining a constant pressure against the fretboard. Also, avoid excessively "plucking" the lower-sounding strings by holding them quiet with your right hand.

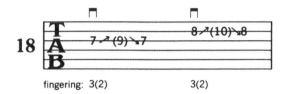

Practice two-fret bends and releases in the following examples. Make your bends sound like those on the audio.

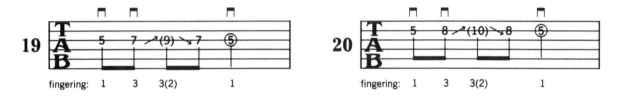

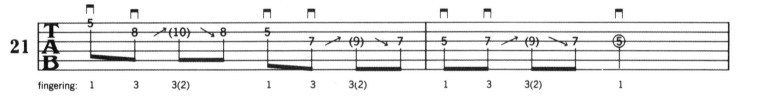

When the rhythm notation stem appears only on the target pitch and not on the initial note, an *immediate bend* is indicated. Pick the note and bend it up right away to the target pitch.

> TIP: When a bend shows no release, yet it is followed by a note on a different string, the string must be released without actually hearing the release. To do this, remove the pressure of your bend slightly so the string becomes muted right at the same moment that you pick the next note.

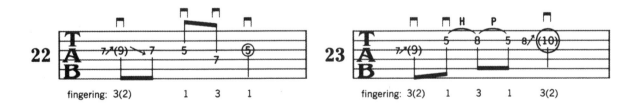

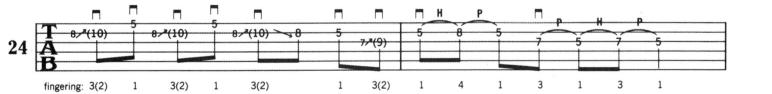

ROCK CLICHÉS 7

The following patterns appear so commonly in rock and metal lead guitar that they are sometimes called *clichés*. They may be used as building blocks for longer lead phrases. Practice each cliché until you can make them sound just like on the audio.

TIP: For the first cliché below, lay your first finger flat across both the first and second strings, extending the fingertip slightly so that it lightly touches the unbent third string. That way, the third string will stay quiet when you lift your third finger off the fretboard after each bend.

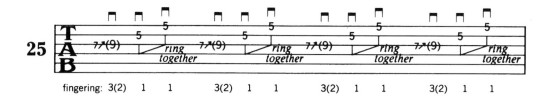

TIP: Make sure that you lift up your reinforcing second finger right *before* the pull-off to the first finger, so it won't be in the way.

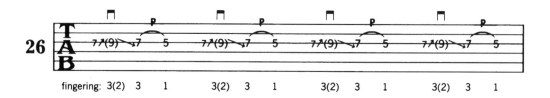

TIP: In example 27, pick the second string just as the bend reaches its target pitch, then let both strings ring out together as you hold the bend.

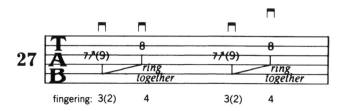

TIP: Example 28 is similar to 27. Just as the bend reaches its target pitch, pick the next note, letting both strings ring together. Then, pick the second string again (still bent) and release.

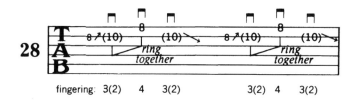

FINGER VIBRATO ◆8◆

Another key component of good lead technique is a strong *finger vibrato*. Consisting of a series of quick bends and releases, it makes the notes sound much more exciting and gives them better sustain.

This type of finger vibrato is actually accomplished by twisting the wrist more than moving the fingers. Press the side of the knuckle of your first finger against the bottom edge of the fretboard, and pivot your hand as shown in the photos. Vibrato is indicated by a ∿ symbol.

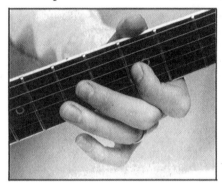
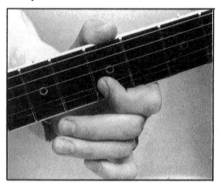

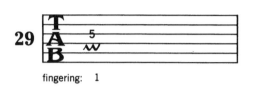

fingering: 1

Below, vibrato is applied to the minor pentatonic scale. To achieve vibrato on the sixth string, pull down for the bends. On the first string, push up. All other strings may be either pushed up or pulled down.

> TIP: First, get a smooth, controlled, slow vibrato with four distinct bends and releases on each note. Then slowly increase the speed of the bends as you are comfortable.

fingering: 1   4   1   3   1   3   1   3   1   3   1   3   1

Vibrato can also appear on a note that is already bent. For a *vibrato-bend*, push up to the destination pitch, release slightly, then bend back up and release slightly again, over and over. Make sure that each bend reaches the target pitch. This is a more difficult vibrato technique. Just be patient and keep working at it!

> TIP: First, try to get two distinct bend/release sequences for each vibrato bend. Then go for three. When you can do that, make it four and slowly increase the tempo.

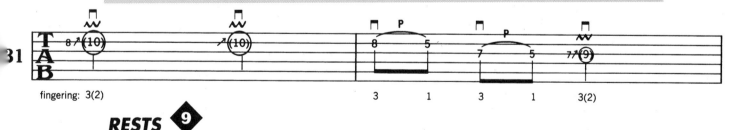

fingering: 3(2)   3   1   3   1   3(2)

RESTS ◆9◆

A rest is a space of time where no notes are played. In other words, silence. Stop the strings and hold them quiet for the duration of any rests. (If you'd like more practice reading and playing rests, see Metal Rhythm Guitar Volume 1.)

count: 1   2   3   4   1   &   2   &   3   4

13

RHYTHMIC PATTERNS ◆10◆

Often a simple cliché may be turned into an interesting lead phrase using rhythmic patterns. First, listen to example 33 to get a feel for the rhythm. Then play it, tapping out the beat steadily with your foot. The first note lands on the downbeat of one, and the next note is on the "&" of beat two.

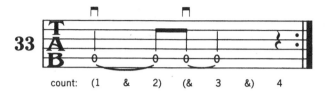

Below, a three note cliché is applied to this rhythm. Since notes that fall on a beat are naturally emphasized more to the ear, notice how the rhythm naturally accents different notes as the three note sequence repeats.

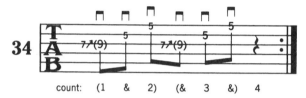

Example 35, below, shows a common two-measure rhythm. Notice that both of the licks that follow in examples 36 and 37 use this same rhythm.

> TIP: Make sure you tap you foot steadily with the underlying *beat* and not with the repeating note pattern, or this rhythmic effect will be somewhat lost.

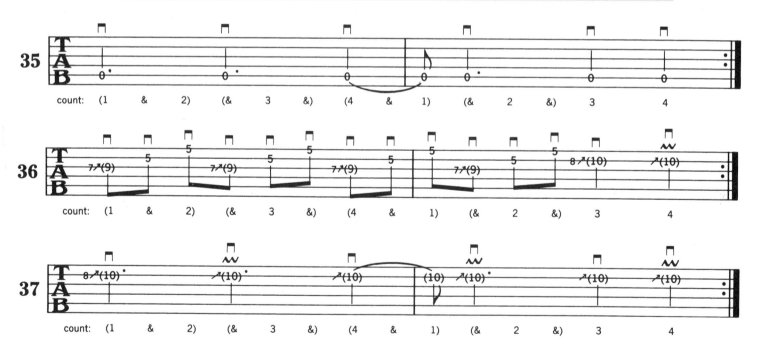

Now try creating a few similar riffs of your own, by plugging different cliché patterns into the rhythmic pattern show in example 35.

14

MINOR PENTATONIC RIFFS 🔶11🔶

The following riffs are two-measure A minor pentatonic phrases which incorporate the techniques covered so far, including hammer-ons and pull-offs, two-fret bends and releases, rock clichés, vibrato, and rhythmic patterns. After you have memorized the sound and the visual pattern of each riff, tap your foot along with the count or play along with a metronome.

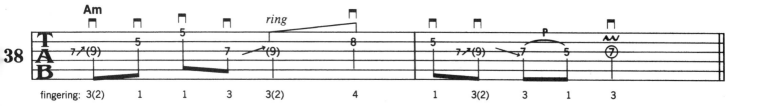

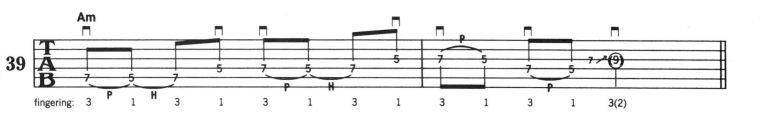

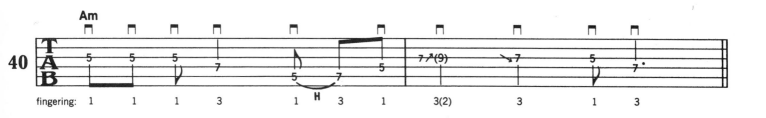

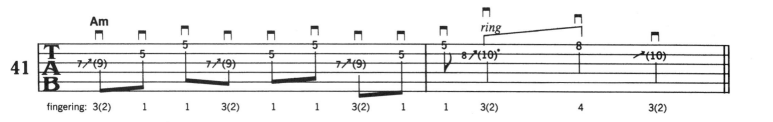

SPECIAL ARTICULATIONS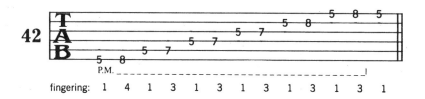
Palm Muting

Palm muting creates a percussive, muffled tone if played cleanly or with low distortion. With heavy distortion it gives notes a thicker, bassier sound and a strong "crunch." Lay the fleshy part of your right hand palm over the bridge saddles, covering just a bit of the end of the strings. Palm muting is indicated by the symbol "P.M." (See Metal Rhythm Guitar Volume 1, or Thrash Metal Guitar for more practice with palm muting.)

Artificial Harmonics

Artificial harmonics turn ordinary notes into high-pitched, attention-getting screams, or squeals. They are also sometimes called false harmonics, pick harmonics, or pinch harmonics since they are created with a specific type of picking technique. They are especially effective when played with heavy distortion and an aggressive finger vibrato.

Hold your pick fairly close to the tip and turn it so that part of your thumb slightly touches the string as you pick. Touching the string lightly as it is picked creates the harmonic. Then move your thumb away from the string immediately so as not to deaden it. Artificial harmonics are indicated by a small "A" with the fret number in a diamond. (For more on this technique, see Metal Guitar Tricks.)

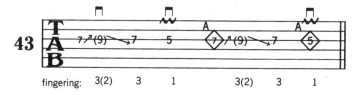

The Slide

The following examples illustrate the slide. After you play the note, slide your finger down and off the neck. You shouldn't hear any distinct pitch apart from the original note.

To slide up to a note, do the exact opposite. Pick the string as you touch the fretboard, and then slide up to the note. Make sure that your hand is moving as you touch the fretboard, or you will hear an unwanted note first, and then the slide.

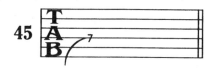

The "Blues" Bend

The "blues" bend is a bend at the tail end of a note. Your ear doesn't so much register it as a pitch change, instead it simply creates a certain effect, or feel. Below, first the notes are played without this "blues" bend, and then they are played with it. Listen for the effect it gives the notes. To bend, pull the string down with your first finger. No target pitch is given because it doesn't really matter exactly how far you bend.

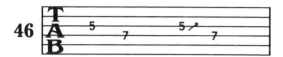

These bluesy-sounding bends are not always indicated in the following licks and solos, as you can and should give the music your own interpretation. If every minute detail were notated exactly, there would be so much information it would become overwhelming. And worse, that level of detail would tend to suggest that you must play it exactly as written or it isn't "right." Let's leave some room for your creativity. Listen carefully and rely on your own ears to tell you what sounds good and what doesn't. Remember, there is no "right" or "wrong." All that matters is, does it sound good? So practice these type of bends along with the other Special Articulations to incorporate them into your playing technique and use them whenever and where ever you think they sound cool!

RIFFS USING THE SPECIAL ARTICULATIONS

The following riffs use all of the special articulations, including palm-muting, artificial harmonics, slight "blues" bends, and slides up and down. Examples 48 and 49 have pick-up notes, that is, notes which begin before and lead into the first measure of the phrase.

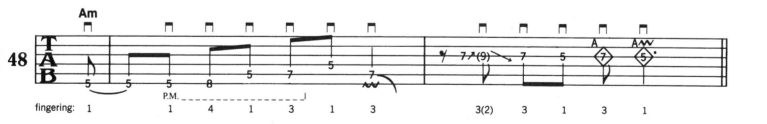

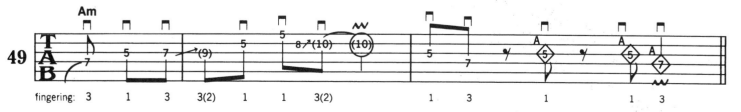

17

"Open Fire" features a lead solo over a backing rhythm track. It follows the form ABABA, with A representing the opening riff (or theme) and B representing the solo sections. So first you'll hear the theme (A) followed by the solo (B). Then it repeats the A and B section, this time without the lead guitar, so you can practice over the rhythm track.

The solo, transcribed below, utilizes just the A minor pentatonic scale with all of the techniques presented in Chapter 1. The phrases are numbered 1-8. Practice each of them separately before putting them all together. Then, after you've got it down, try substituting different lead phrases to create your own solos to play over the backing rhythm track.

OPEN FIRE 14
(Solo #1)

CHAPTER 2
NOTES ON THE SIXTH STRING

To play in different keys, you must know the names of the notes on the sixth string. The pattern repeats at the twelfth fret. The names are the same, but all are one octave higher.

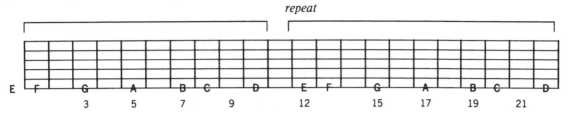

A sharp sign (♯) raises a note one fret and a flat sign (♭) lowers a note one fret. Therefore, each fret space above that is not labelled can actually have two names. For example, the note at the fourth fret may be called either G♯ or A♭, depending on the context.

CHANGING KEYS 15

All of the licks shown so far have been in the A minor pentatonic scale (in the key of A minor). To solo in other keys, simply slide the scale pattern up or down the neck, placing the root note of the scale pattern on the new keynote. The licks below are in the keys of G minor and B minor.

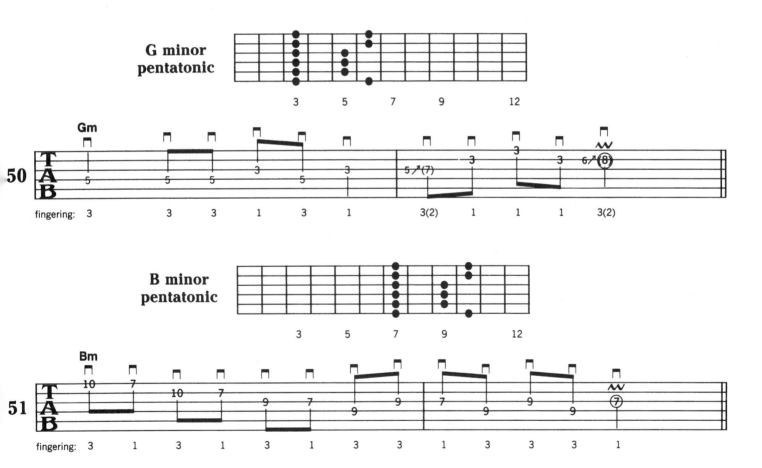

19

THE OCTAVE POSITION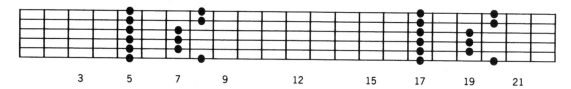

Another common form for the minor pentatonic scale is called the octave position. If you move any note up twelve frets, it will be one octave higher. Therefore, the A minor pentatonic scale form repeats identically, beginning at the 17th fret. The lick in example 52 uses this higher, octave position.

A minor pentatonic

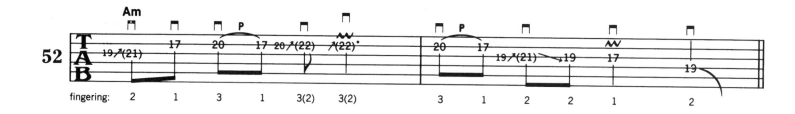

THE DIAGONAL FORM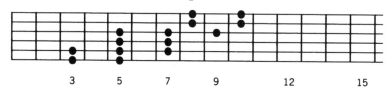

The extended form of the A minor pentatonic scale shown below moves diagonally through several different positions. Notice how many of the notes are the same as in the basic position, with a low extension at the bottom and a high extension at the top. A *slide* between notes is played by holding the finger against the fretboard and shifting up or down to the next note. This is indicated by a line between notes. It may or may not be picked.

A minor pentatonic

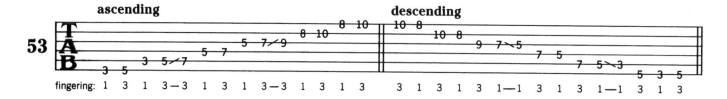

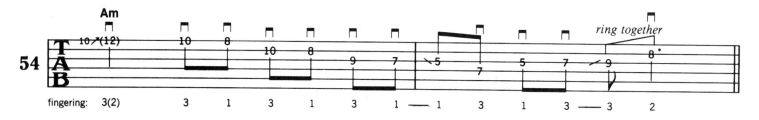

ALTERNATE PICKING AND SIXTEENTH NOTES

Alternate picking is a technique whereby the strokes of the pick alternate down and up, allowing notes to be picked twice as fast without any additional movement. This essential skill can be found in the lightning-fast runs of guitarists like Paul Gilbert, Steve Vai, and Kirk Hammet, as well as many other rock and metal players today.

Here, we will first establish the foundation for a uniform alternate picking format, starting with sixteenth note rhythms. Then we'll expand and develop this approach throughout the method. (For an even more detailed breakdown of alternate picking, also see Speed Mechanics for Lead Guitar.)

The sixteenth notes below use a consistent alternating motion of the pick. Notice that each beat begins with a *downstroke*.

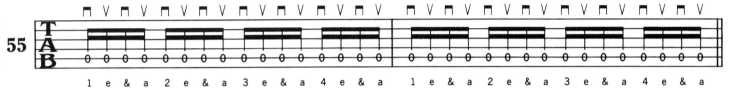

When two sixteenths are tied, they may be substituted with an eighth note. Skip the string for the tied sixteenth, but do not alter the picking pattern of the other notes. Each downbeat still gets a downstroke. (If you have trouble with these rhythms, refer to Metal Rhythm Guitar Volume 2 for more practice.)

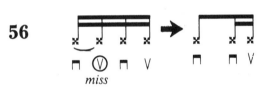

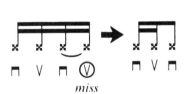

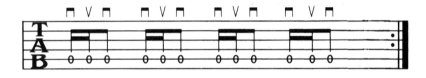

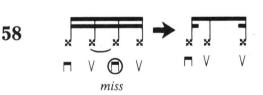

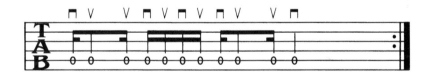

Three tied sixteenth notes last 3/4 of a beat, and may be substituted with a dotted eighth note.

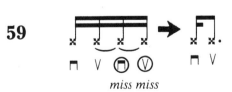

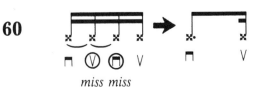

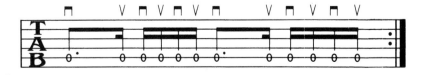

Below, a rhythm is first shown, followed by a lick which uses that rhythm. After you have these licks down, try creating a lick of your own that uses each rhythm.

TIP: First practice the rhythm with just the right hand, to get a feel for the alternating picking. Then try the lick, which is picked exactly the same.

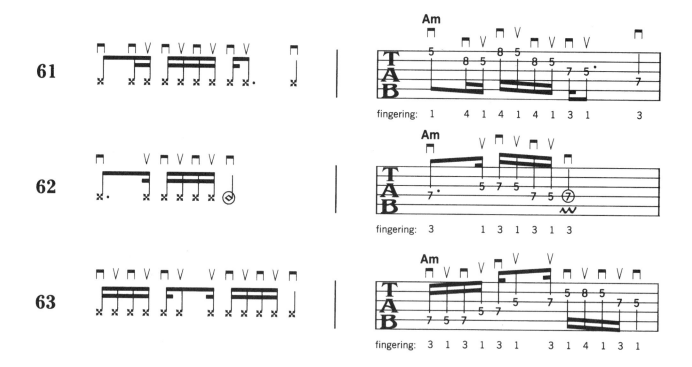

If a note is played with a hammer-on, pull-off, bend, or release, skip the picking of that note, but do not alter the picking pattern of the other notes. The symbol ✔ means to repeat the preceding figure.

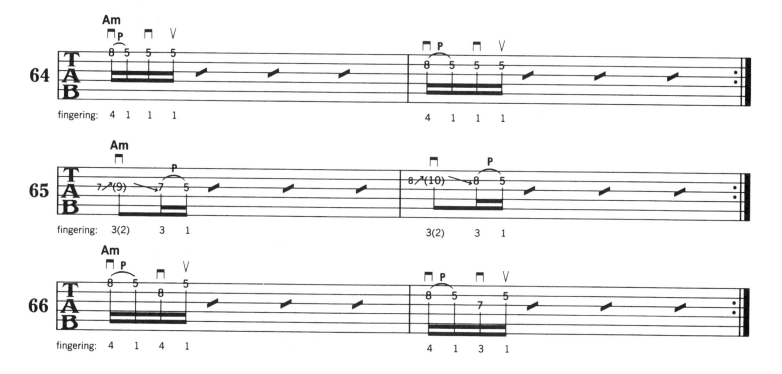

22

SPEED EXERCISES 🔹19

Speed exercises are used throughout the method to build accuracy and synchronization, and to prepare you for various solos. First listen to each exercise and learn the notes. When you have the left hand part memorized, then move to the right hand and concentrate on the correct right-hand picking. After you have the pattern "under your fingers" fairly well, you are ready to begin practicing it as a speed exercise:

- Begin slowly and evenly, gradually increasing the speed until it gets to be as fast as you can play accurately and comfortably.
- Push your speed up just a little bit more. And as you do, concentrate on smoothing it out by making smaller, more relaxed motions. (The natural tendency is to tense up. What you want to do is bring down your level of tension while you maintain your speed.)
- Repeat each measure four or more times, then raise everything up one fret and repeat. Continue all the way up and back down the fretboard.
- Go on to the next exercise and do the same thing!

As you can see, the six exercises below can take quite a lot of time to practice this way! But it will pay off when you turn to the next page.

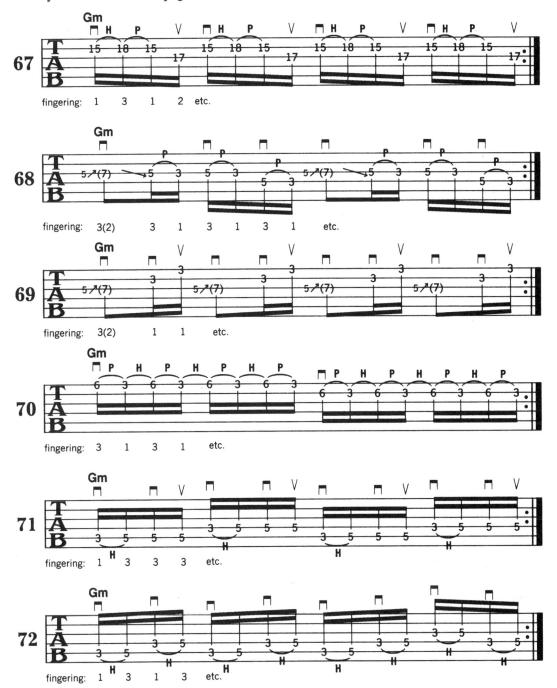

23

"**To The Stage**" is our second lead solo over a backing rhythm track. Again it uses the same ABABA form as before, with the B sections for the solos. The transcribed solo, below, features fast, repeating sixteenth note patterns arranged in four, four-measure phrases. Practice each phrase separately before putting it all together. Also, don't forget to use the second B section to play the solo over the rhythm track, to improvise, or to compose your own solo.

TO THE STAGE ◆20
(Solo #2)

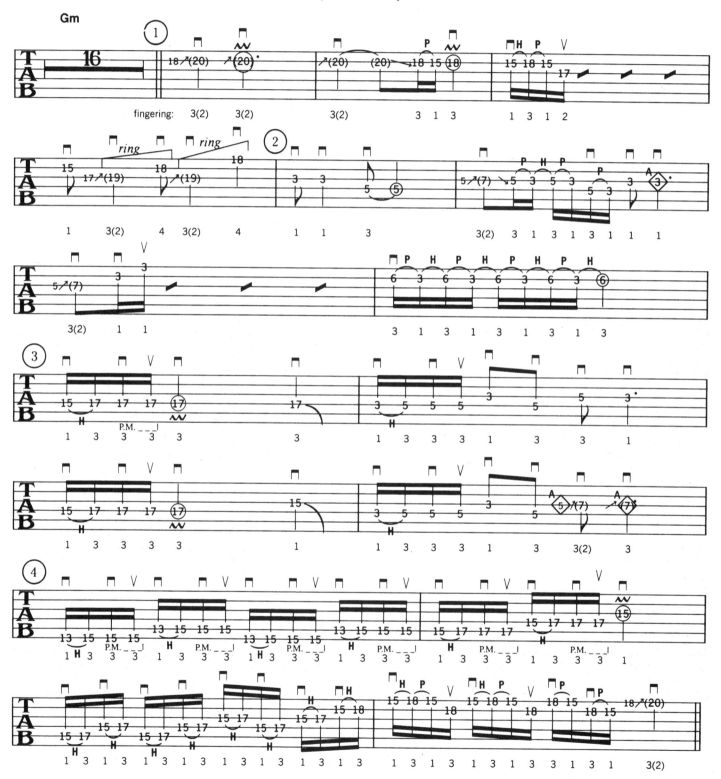

CHAPTER 3
THE BLUES SCALE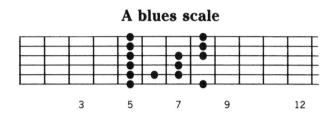

The so-called "blues" scale is a minor pentatonic scale with one additional note. Below, that added note appears in two places within the A minor pentatonic shape.

A blues scale

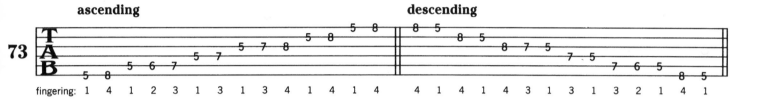

In the short lick below, this additional note of the blues scale is marked with an asterisk (*) each place it appears.

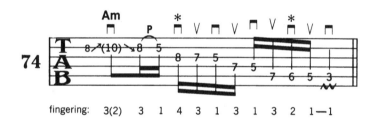

THE ONE-FRET BEND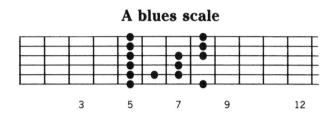

This new note of the blues scale can be reached by bending the next lower note up one fret, or a half-step. In lick 75, notice the difference between the two-fret and one-fret bends.

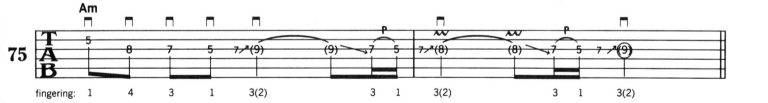

TRIPLETS 23

Eighth note triplets are three notes evenly spaced in one beat. When they are played with alternate picking, the first group of triplets will start with a downstroke and the second beat will begin on an upstroke. Make sure your picking is correct as you tap your foot along with the beat in example 76.

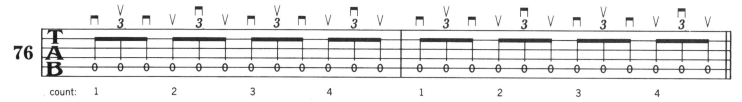

The following licks, in Am, Gm and Em, use alternate picking with eighth note triplets.

TIP: First listen to each lick and memorize the left hand patterns of the notes, by playing with all downstrokes. When you have that much of it memorized, then concentrate fully on the alternate picking.

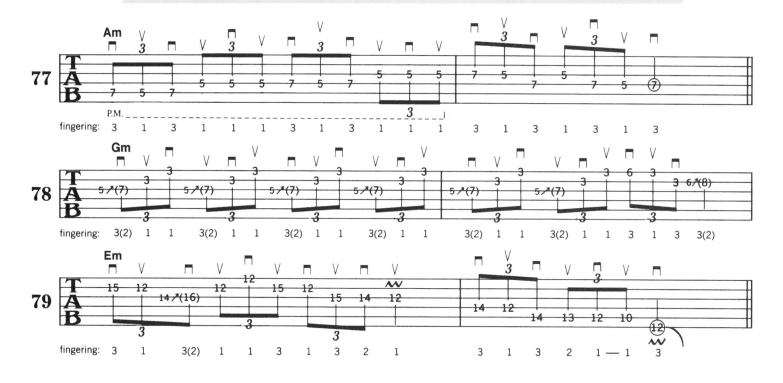

A *swing*, or *shuffle* rhythm is a kind of triplet based rhythm, made by tieing the first two notes of each triplet together. The two tied eighths are written as a quarter note, and take up 2/3 of the beat (♫ = ♩♪). This rhythm is easiest to pick with a downstroke on each beat.

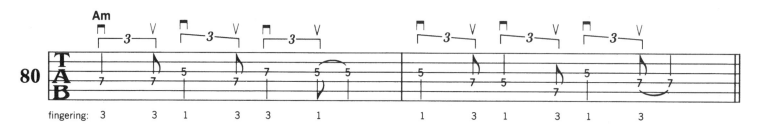

26

If the second and third notes of a series of triplet groups are each played with hammers, pulls, or bends, again, pick with a downstroke on each beat.

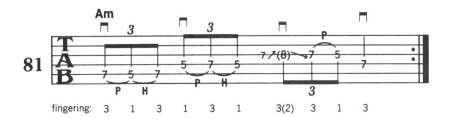

Notice that some of the notes "sandwiched" within the triplets below are not found in the minor pentatonic or blues scale. These incidental notes are called *passing notes*, or *passing tones*. They may act as a sort of "melodic lubricant" and smooth out the run. Again, notice the downstroke picking approach.

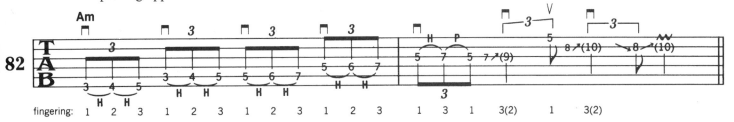

Licks 83 and 84 combine all of these triplet picking approaches, with some alternate picking, some hammer-ons, pull-offs, bends, and a bit of the swing rhythm, and some passing tones.

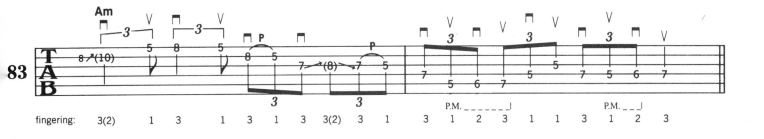

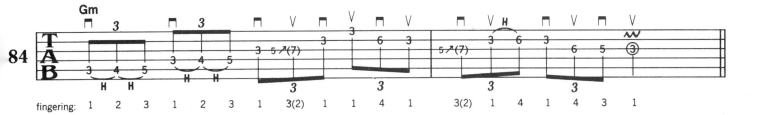

SPECIAL ARTICULATIONS ◆24◆
The Pre-Bend

A pre-bend means that the string is bent up to the target pitch silently and then picked and released. None of the upward bend is heard. Pre-bends are indicated with a "PB" and a downward arrow for the following release. Examples 85 and 86, below, use both regular bends and pre-bends. Notice the difference in how they sound.

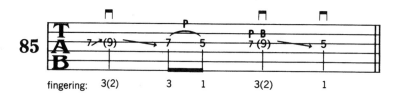

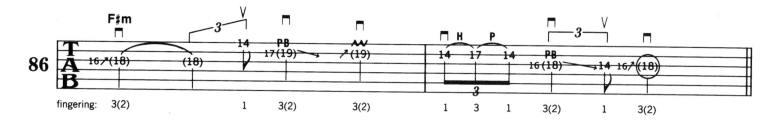

The Slow Bend

There are a multitude of different ways to approach a bend, and different players may bring very different interpretations to it. The subtleties of how fast the string is bent and exactly when it reaches the target pitch, combine to give it a certain feel or character. Again, however, it is difficult to notate all this without being overwhelmed in a tangle of details. Therefore, just the basics are given—that is, the starting point and the target pitch. And it is left up to you to listen carefully to the feel of the bend and copy it by ear. Does it hit the target pitch quickly and energetically? Or does it move up slowly and reach the target pitch only at the very end of the note? Developing this type of bending control is a valuable skill that will radically expand your musical options.

Example 87 uses slow bends, that reach their destination pitch only at the very end of the note. Listen for the tension this creates. And notice the soaring feel of the high bend in the third measure, with it's slow release. After you've got the feel of these bends down, try experiment with other bending approaches and see how different you can make it.

TIP: Make sure you have enough gain (and sustain) so that your note don't die away prematurely. Then you can linger on the bends and not be tempted to rush them.

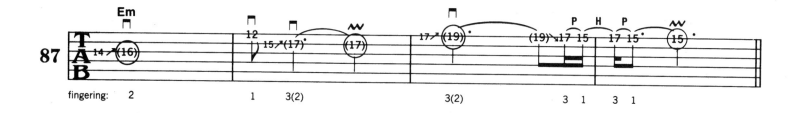

The Rake

Raking the pick over several muted strings as you strike a note creates a thicker, more definite attack on the note. To get the position for this, lightly touch and mute all the strings with the first finger of your left hand, and adopt a palm-mute position for the right hand. The strings will give only a percussive click with no definite pitch. Now, rake the pick across the strings, lifting the right hand palm-mute as you reach the final note.

Staccato

Notes that are played very short and abrupt are *staccato*. This is indicated by a dot placed directly above or below a note. Pick the note normally, but immediately stop the string with both hands. When staccato appears on a bent note, stop the string quickly as it reaches its target pitch.

QUARTER NOTE TRIPLETS ◆25◆

Quarter note triplets are three notes evenly spaced within *two* beats. They give a certain staggered, or lazy feeling. Listen to get the feel and then play along with the audio. (For more practice with these and other types of more advanced rhythms, see Metal Rhythm Guitar Volume 2 and Speed Mechanics for Lead Guitar, Part Two.) Also, lay your first finger flat to play two-string double-stops in example 92.

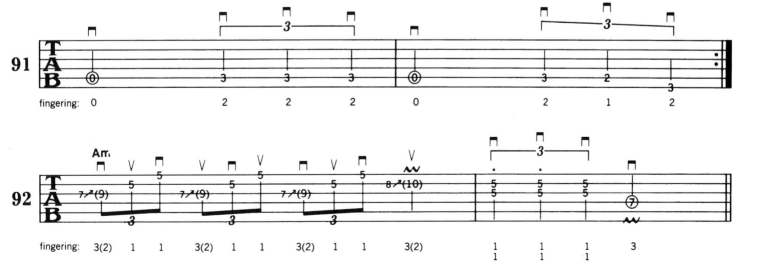

Eddie Van Halen

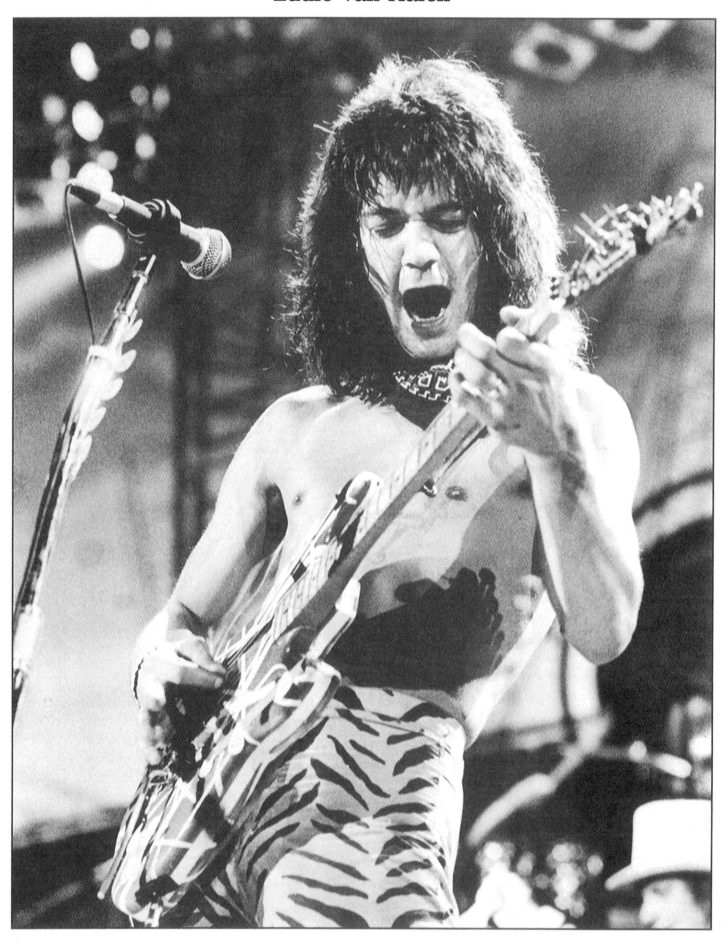

Photo by: Bill Warren/Star File

Randy Rhoads

Photo by: William E. Basstone/Star File

An improvised solo is one that is spontaneously created on the spot. Many experienced lead players find that their improvisations tend to be fresher and more exciting than preplanned and composed solos. However, if you have a rather limited amount of licks to draw from, it is likely that all of your solos will end up sounding somewhat alike. To avoid this horrible fate and to keep things interesting, let's take a look at *phrasing*.

A *phrase* is a musical thought. Just as a single word doesn't convey a full thought, neither does a single note. It is only when words (or notes) are combined in meaningful sequences that we have a complete thought. So a phrase is a complete, self-contained musical thought, much like a sentence. And to continue our analogy, just as sentences are arranged one after another to tell a story, musical phrases are combined to form a musical story. In this case, our musical story happens to be a guitar solo.

Below, a one measure rhythm is shown, followed by two different licks which both use this same rhythm. After you play these licks, create a few more of your own using this same rhythm.

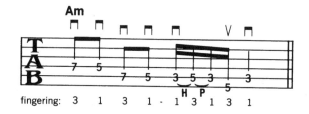

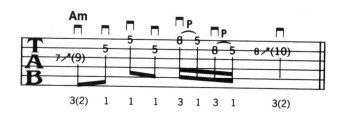

Example 94 shows another one bar rhythm, followed by two licks. After you play them, see how many different licks you can improvise using this same rhythm.

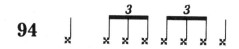

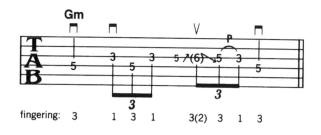

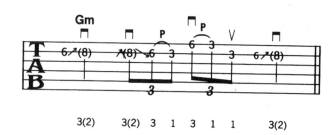

Now let's try it with two bar phrases. Again, after you learn the licks in each of the following examples, make up a few of your own using these rhythms as guides. If you find that you want to change the rhythm to suite your lick, go for it. Remember, these are just a springboard to get you going and to give you a feel for the length of the two bar phrase.

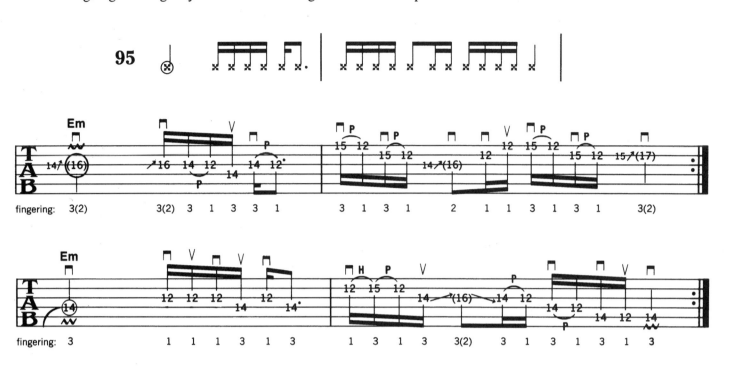

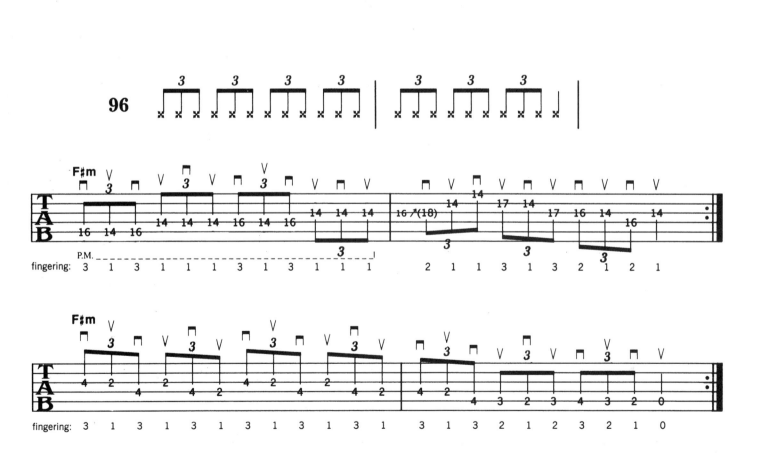

Focusing on rhythms like this, and then combining them with different notes can give a nearly endless number of possibilities. Keep practicing these examples and creating new licks of your own until you can *feel* the length of the phrases and no longer have to count them out or stick with preplanned rhythms.

"From the Heart" is a slow metal-blues shuffle in the key of F#m. The solo, transcribed below, features all the different bending approaches as well as all of the special articulation nuances covered. The phrasing is not as straightforward as in the previous solo, with pick-up notes leading into phrase one, the second and third phrases run together, and phrase three extends over into the start of phrase four. Listen for these irregularities. And after you get the solo down, don't forget to practice your improvisation! This is the perfect track to practice laid-back blues-type improvs.

FROM THE HEART 27
(Solo #3)

CHAPTER 4
NOTES ON THE FIFTH STRING

To play in different keys using the following scale form with the root on the fifth string (shown below), you must first know the names of the notes. Play up and down through the notes shown below, saying the names out loud until you have them memorized.

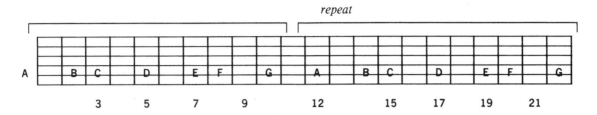

As before, the notes in the unlabeled spaces above are named with sharp and flat signs. Remember, sharp = up one fret, and flat = down one fret. Also, notice that all the natural notes (those that are not sharp or flat) are a whole step, or two frets apart except B, C and E, F which are only a half step, or one fret apart.

MINOR PENTATONIC (FIFTH STRING ROOT) 28

The A5 power chord at the 12th fret is shown below, with its root on the fifth string. Notice how it fits into the A minor pentatonic form shown below.

A5 power chord

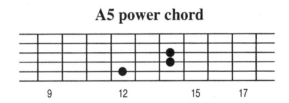

A minor pentatonic

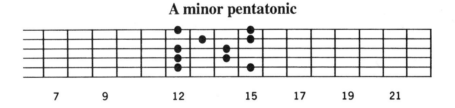

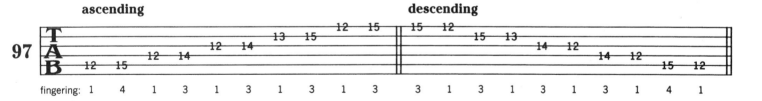

The lick below uses the same position as the E minor pentatonic shape learned earlier, but here we are in the key of A *minor*. Take care to note the difference.

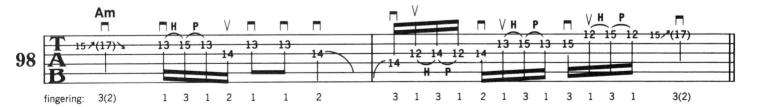

SCALE TONES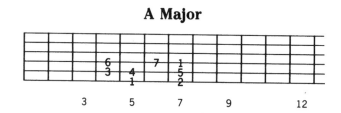

The notes of the major scale are numbered 1, 2, 3, 4, 5, 6, 7, and these numbers are called *tones*. The eighth tone, or octave, is numbered with a 1 since it is the same letter name as the first note (A).

A Major

If you were to continue up or down this scale, the same sequence of tones would repeat over again, with all the notes exactly one octave higher or lower, respectively. A seven-tone scale, like the major scale shown above, is called a *diatonic* scale.

Keep in mind that these numbered tones reflect the position of a note in relation to the root note of the scale, which in this case is A. The term *note*, on the other hand, refers to a specific pitch with a letter name, like A, E, or F♯. So the note A is tone 1, or the root, in A major. But in G major, the note G will become tone 1, the root.

Admittedly, the pure major scale is quite rarely used in metal. But the steps of every other scale are numbered in relation it, so that's where we begin. The darker natural minor scale (or pure minor scale) is another diatonic scale that *is* quite common in metal. Natural minor is the same as the major scale except that the 3rd, 6th, and 7th steps are flatted, or lowered one fret. So the tones of natural minor are 1, 2, ♭3, 4, 5, ♭6, ♭7.

A natural minor

or,

A natural minor

Of course different people may have somewhat different impressions, but most would agree that the major scale feels basically bright, happy, light, and triumphant. The minor scale, on the other hand, feels dark, sad, heavy, or medieval.

99 Listen to the mood of a melody in a **major** scale.

100 Listen to the mood of a melody in a **minor** scale.

Each different type of scale has its own distinct feel, or mood. However, in our Western system of tonality, major and minor are regarded as polar opposites and given "priority status."

MINOR PENTATONIC TONES ◆30◆

The term *pentatonic* means "five-tone," so a minor pentatonic scale is a five-tone minor scale. Leave out the 2nd and 6th steps from the natural minor scale, and you have the minor pentatonic scale.

A natural minor

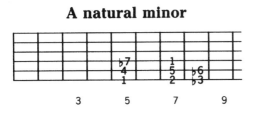

A minor pentatonic

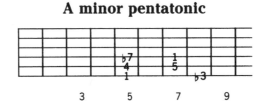

Knowing the tones you are playing is even more important than knowing the note names because the tonal numbering gives each note's relationship to the root. And it is this relationship that gives any note its particular effect. For instance, the minor seventh tone, or ♭7, will always give the same type of sound regardless of what key it is in.

Learning these tones is the first step. You're on a path to develop your ear so that you'll eventually recognize these different interval relationships just by their sound. This is called having *relative pitch*. Ultimately, this skill will help you learn by ear much more quickly, and translate melodies to the guitar much more easily. So, let's get started by memorizing the tones within the basic minor pentatonic shape.

A minor pentatonic tones

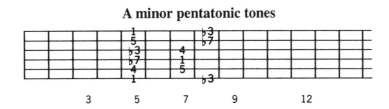

After you learn the following riffs, write in the numbered tone of each note in the blank underneath the tab. The additional note of the blues scale is a ♭5, or *diminished 5th*. It is also included below. The answers appear on page 40.

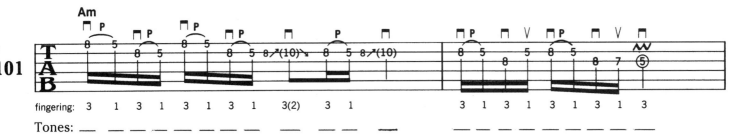

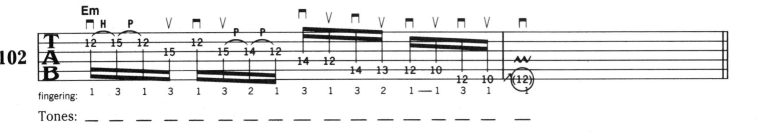

Below, the tones of the minor pentatonic form with the root on the fifth string are shown. Notice the similarity of the tones and their shape, as compared with the other minor pentatonic shape.

A minor pentatonic tones

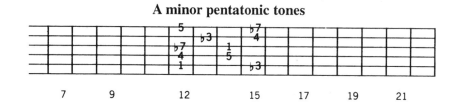

The lick in example 103 uses this form of A minor pentatonic. Again, write in the tones in the spaces underneath each note. Answers on page 40.

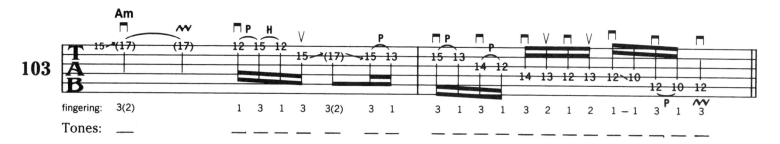

THE NATURAL MINOR SCALE AND TONES 31

Below, the dots show the minor pentatonic shape that you already know. By adding the tones 2 and ♭6 back into the scale, we fill out the natural minor scale. It is important that you can not only play the pentatonic and natural minor scales, but that you can also see how they are superimposed together.

A natural minor

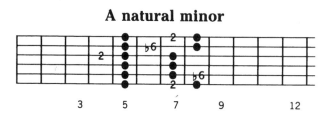

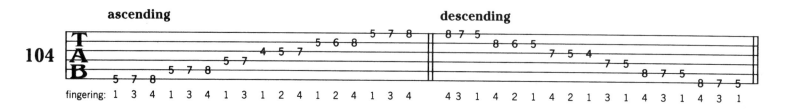

38

The licks in examples 105 and 106 combine notes of the natural minor scale with a basically pentatonic/blues approach. Write in the tones underneath each note. Answers on page 40.

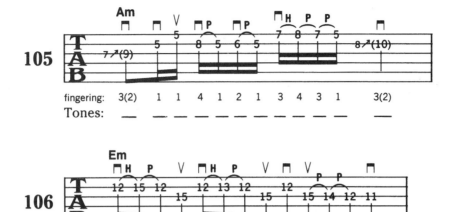

Next is the natural minor form with its root on the fifth string. Again, notice the pentatonic pattern within the scale. You want to be able to visualize both patterns, seeing graphically which notes are shared in common. Write in the tones underneath each note. Answers on page 40.

A natural minor

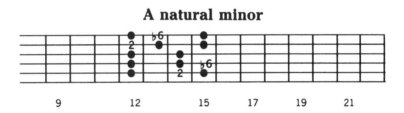

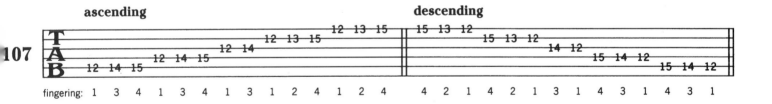

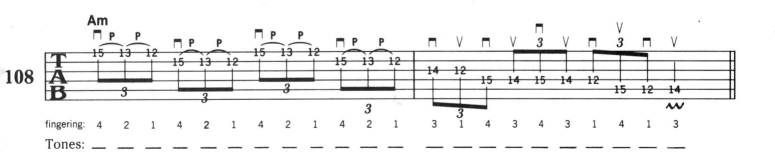

Tones:

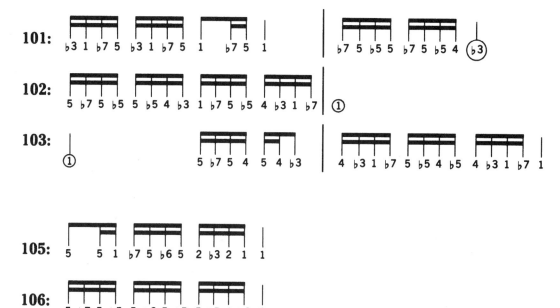

101: ♭3 1 ♭7 5 ♭3 1 ♭7 5 1 ♭7 5 1 | ♭7 5 ♭5 5 ♭7 5 ♭5 4 (♭3)

102: 5 ♭7 5 ♭5 5 ♭5 4 ♭3 1 ♭7 5 ♭5 4 ♭3 1 ♭7 | ①

103: ① | 5 ♭7 5 4 5 4 ♭3 | 4 ♭3 1 ♭7 5 ♭5 4 ♭5 4 ♭3 1 ♭7 1

105: 5 5 1 ♭7 5 ♭6 5 2 ♭3 2 1 1

106: 5 ♭7 5 ♭5 5 ♭6 5 ♭5 5 ♭5 4 ♭3 2

108: ³ ♭7 ♭6 5 ³ 4 ♭3 2 ³ ♭7 ♭6 5 ³ 4 ♭3 2 | ³ 1 ♭7 ♭6 ³ 5 ♭6 5 ³ 4 ♭3 1 2

SPEED EXERCISES 32

The following speed exercises will help to prepare you for the next solo, as well as develop greater articulation, control and accuracy. Again, practice them as before, on page 23.

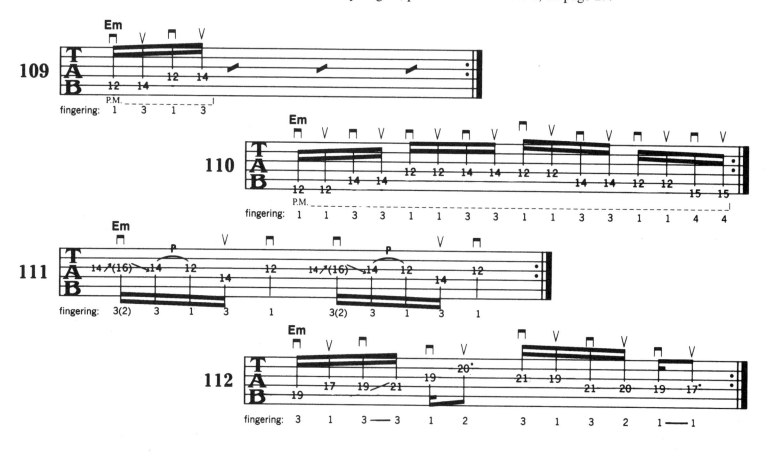

"The Heavy Side" uses classic heavy metal progressions in E minor, pedalling the palm-muted, low E string in the main rhythm riff. The solo, with four fairly straightforward 4-bar phrases and 16th note figures, is strong and driving. Overall, it begins in the middle register, drops lower in the second phrase, raises up for the third phrase with a repeating pattern that builds intensity, and finally rises to a climax in phrase four at the high E bend. The rhythm track follows the ABABA form.

THE HEAVY SIDE ◆33◆
(Solo #4)

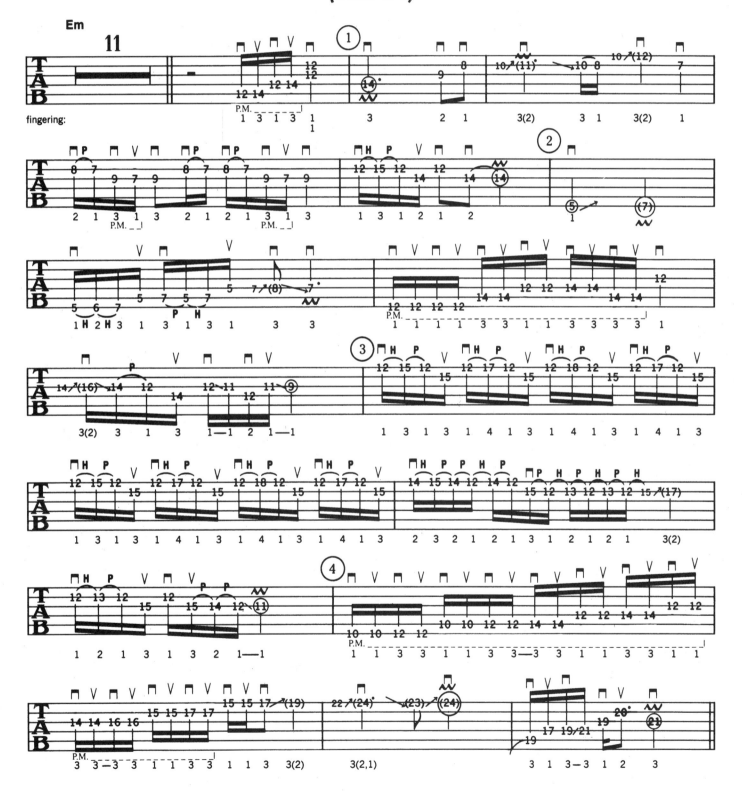

CHAPTER 5
CROSS-STRING PICKING MECHANICS

Many top players, including Zakk Wilde, Steve Vai, Paul Gilbert, Diamond Darrell and others, show off lightning-fast runs in which every note is picked smoothly and with complete synchronization between the left and right hands. Maintaining this consistent alternate picking when you cross back and forth between strings—and keeping it smooth at top speed—is one of the toughest skills to master. But, like everything else, its just a matter of practice. So let's get to it!

> TIP: Practice each of the examples on this page as a speed exercise. Remember—to play faster, concentrate on making smaller motions using just the tip of pick.

With two notes on each string, example 113 crosses between strings leading with a downstroke each time.

113

The next two patterns mix it up a little. But they share something in common, and that is an *inward picking motion*. As you play examples 114 and 115, notice that your pick strikes the strings in the direction shown by the arrows in the photo.

114

115

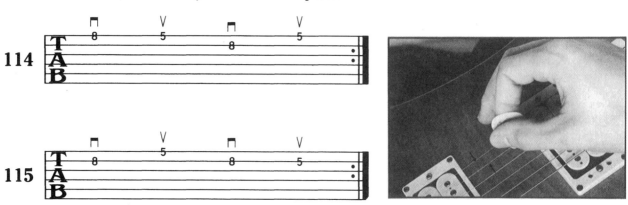

Examples 116 and 117 use the opposite motion, or an *outward picking motion*. As you play them, notice how the motion of your pick corresponds to the arrows.

116

117

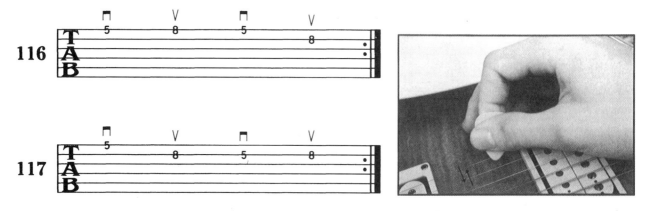

You may find that you have trouble with one particular pattern more than another. If so, practice it repeatedly to work it out. You can also string together the shapes you play best, to capitalize on your strengths and come up with your most impressive runs.

SCALE SEQUENCING AND CONTOURING ◆35◆

If you started on the bottom rung of a ladder and climbed up four steps, then jumped back down three, up four steps and down three, etc., you would move up the ladder one step at a time. If you numbered the rungs, the pattern would be 1234, 2345, 3456, etc. Applying a repeating pattern like this to a scale is known as *sequencing* the scale.

Some typical sequences for scales are:

      1234, 2345, 3456, 4567, 5678, etc.

      1231, 2342, 3453, 4564, 5675, etc.

      123, 234, 345, 456, 567, 678, etc.

      13, 24, 35, 46, 57, 68, etc.

They may also be used descending and they may be inverted to create more possibilities. There are virtually an endless number of possible sequence patterns.

Sequencing exercises will help you to think of grouping notes in a variety of new ways, as well as being great cross-string picking practice. The four examples below break down the first full sequence on the following page into manageable sections. The scale is the A natural minor, sequenced with the first pattern above. First play each example with all downstrokes until you have the notes memorized. Then focus your attention on your right hand as you introduce alternate picking.

> TIP: If you have trouble keeping the picking consistent, try exaggerating the picking motion by making very large movements at first. Then, after you get the knack of it, pare it back down to small, relax picking motions.

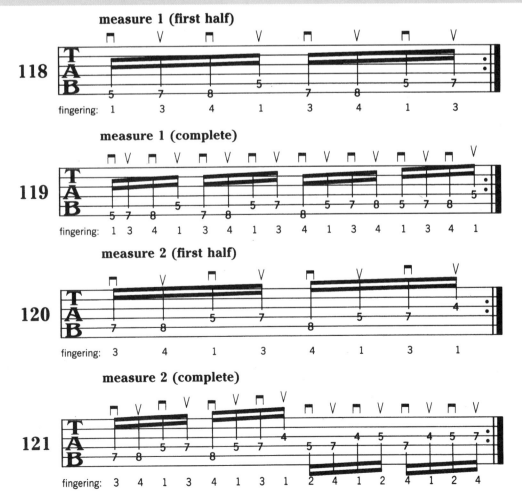

43

Below is the A natural minor scale sequenced in ascending groups of four. Notice that at the end, the sequence is broken to make it wind around and land on the root. This is an example of *contouring*. A contour is a more general term that refers to any shape, while a sequence is only a regular, repeating shape. All sequences are contours, but not all contours are sequences.

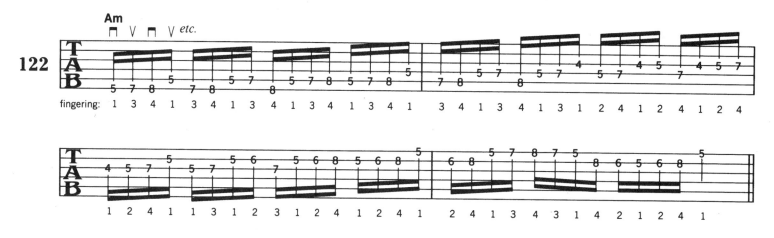

Now let's try a few different sequences with this same scale. The first one below takes the previous sequence pattern, descending and inverted. The next example uses a 1231, 2342 pattern and inverts it to descend. Also, notice where the sequences have been altered for musical purposes, to complete the phrase with a more natural feel.

Example 125 uses a three note descending sequence, played in triplets.

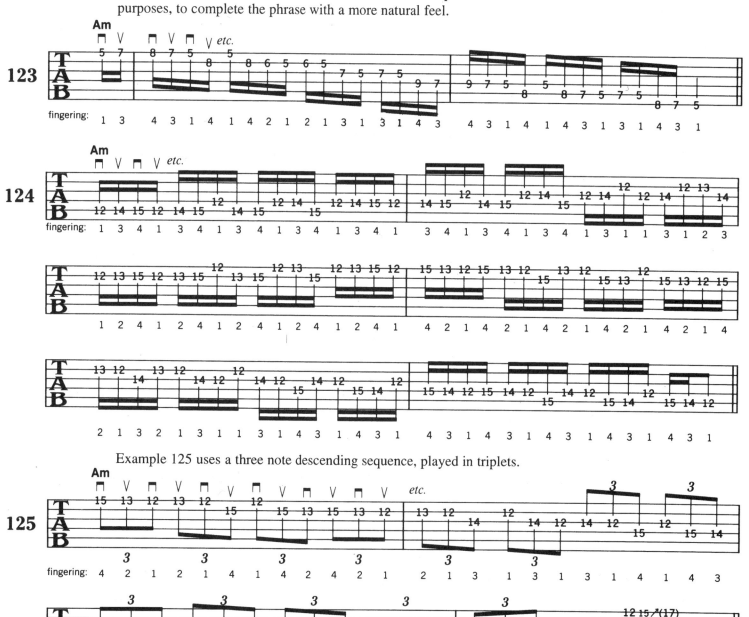

Example 126 uses the two note sequence described on page 43. Again, notice where the pattern is altered to make a more interesting, less mechanical-sounding phrase.

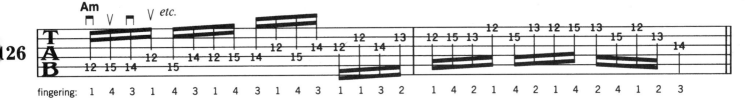

The A minor pentatonic scale is sequenced below. Notice the descending triplet sequence in the first two measures is just like that used in example 125, but here it is applied to a pentatonic shape. In measures three and four—the ascending part—the sequence is changed, forming a Randy Rhoads style pentatonic lick. This sounds good and makes a good exercise, but can you figure out and play the ascending part of the lick using the exact same sequence as the descending part?

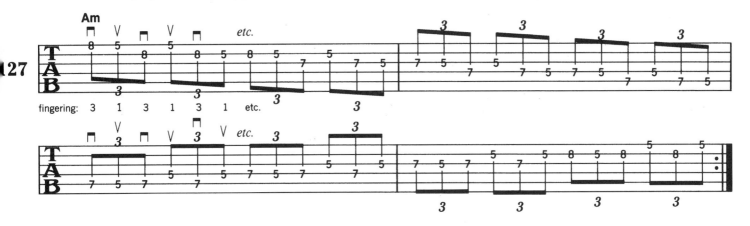

Finally, in example 128, the blues scale is sequenced is descending groups of four. The asterisk (*) marks where you'll need to roll your finger onto the next string to change notes without introducing a break or pause between them.

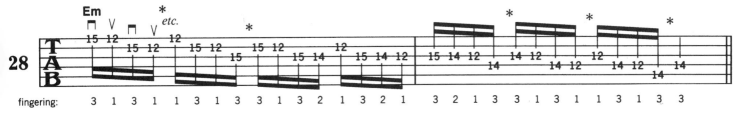

Now, take these sequence exercises and shift them up and down to neck to play in different keys. Playing in different positions of the neck feels different because it requires a different angle to the neck and uses different finger spacing. And there are of course many more sequencing possibilities. Experiment with other sequences and with other scales, too. You can try longer groups of six or even eight notes, or use more convoluted patterns.

129   Listen to a faster eight note sequence

130   Listen to a longer 24-note sequence pattern with subcontours

SCALE SEQUENCING IN LICKS 36

You can use sequences to get more mileage out of your licks. But don't go overboard or your licks may end up sounding like exercises!

Often when you listen to others' fast guitar licks, it may seem like there are more notes in them than there really are. That is to say, a lick may sound as though it has a million notes in it, all over the place, but when you sit down and actually learn it, you find that it uses just one position in and a few familiar patterns. So the moral of the story is to not overdo it with these sequences. They're a great tool for developing technique, but you generally want to blend them in and keep things a little less predictable when it comes to making music. Just be aware of this and listen to what you're playing, and it won't be a problem.

Look for the sequences and contours hiding within the licks below.

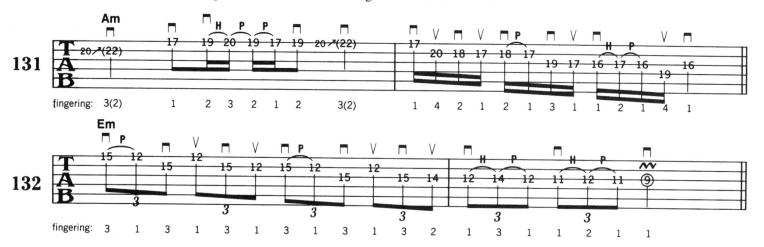

RHYTHMIC PATTERNS 37

Here, as before in Chapter 1, "rhythmic patterns" are created when a set of notes is repeated in such a way that a different note of the pattern falls on each beat. Below, this is accomplished with a six note pattern over sixteenth notes. Notice the natural accents falling on the downbeat of 1, the "&" of 2, and the downbeat of 4.

TIP: Tap your foot along as you play, or the rhythmic effect will be somewhat lost.

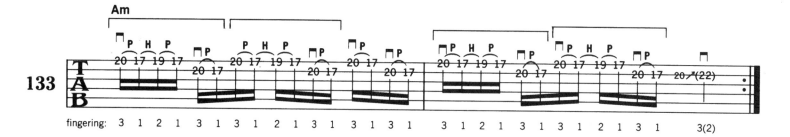

Next is a set of three notes, repeated over sixteenths. Again, tap your foot with the beat.

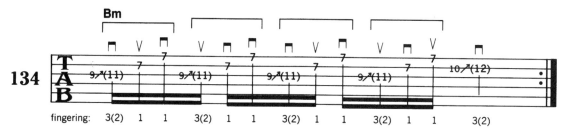

46

THE DORIAN MODE 38

The dorian mode is a seven tone (or diatonic) scale which uses the tones 1, 2, ♭3, 4, 5, 6, ♭7. Since it shares a minor 3rd with the natural minor scale, it is a minor type of scale. In fact, the only different between natural minor and the dorian mode is the 6th step—dorian uses a major 6th. This one half step difference gives the dorian mode a somewhat brighter and less heavy sound as compared to the natural minor scale.

A Dorian mode

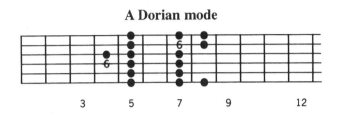

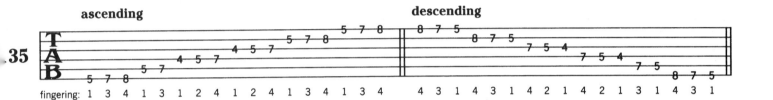

A lot of straightahead, upbeat rock and roll and melodic metal tunes use the dorian mode. Also, the 80's "West coast" lead style of guitarists, championed by the likes of George Lynch and Warren DiMartini, rely heavily on it blended together with the minor pentatonic and blues scales.

The licks below use the dorian mode with a minor pentatonic/blues approach. An asterisk (*) marks each occurrence of dorian's telltale major 6th.

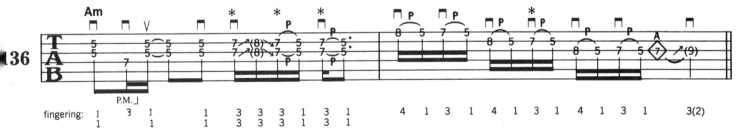

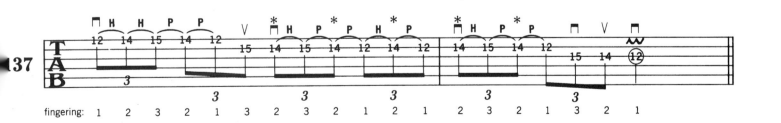

47

SIXTEENTH NOTE TRIPLETS 39

A sixteenth note triplet is three notes played evenly in the space of two sixteenths (or, a half beat). Two of thesetriplets together form a sextuplet, or six notes in one beat. However, it is easier to think of them as triplets—one starting on the downbeat and another starting on the "&". The lick below use sixteenth triplets with passing tones with a pentatonic/blues/dorian approach.

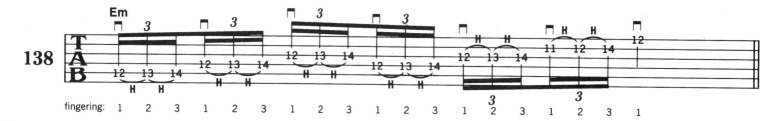

OVERBENDING 40

Two-fret, or whole step bends are the norm, but there's no law against bending further. The licks below incorporate a four-fret bend, which is a distance two whole-steps, and a three-fret bend which is a step and a half. The scale patterns used are to the right with the note being bent and the location of the equivalent target pitch shown in heavy print.

> TIP: First play the note to be bent and target pitch so you know where you're goung. Also, using extra-light guage strings will help to make these mega bends easier.

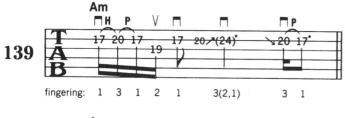

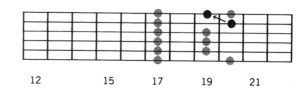

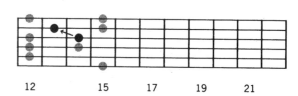

SPEED EXERCISES 41

Again, remember the directions on page 23 for the following Speed Exercises. By now I'm sure you've got them memorized!

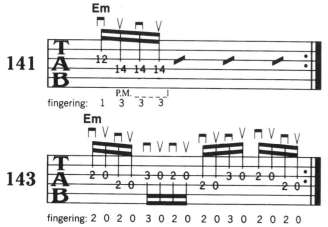

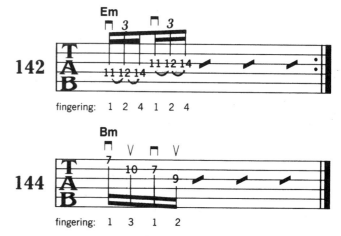

48

"Montezuma's Revenge" may at first seem to paint a decidedly distasteful picture, but don't let these runs psyche you out. True, they'll takes some practice, but persevere. Build it up a little at a time and you just might surprise yourself! Give it a shot, and try to capture some of the urgency in this lead. Also keep up with the key changes, from A dorian in the opening riff, to Em at the solo, and then to Bm for the second half of the solo.

MONTEZUMA'S REVENGE 42
(Solo #5)

CHAPTER 6
NATURAL HARMONICS

The diagram below shows the fundamental vibration of a string.

A string not allowed to move in the middle when it is picked will vibrate like this:

The point in the middle where the string is held motionless is called a *node*. Since the waves are half as large, the frequency doubles and the pitch goes up one octave above the open string. We call this pattern of vibration a *harmonic* of the original vibration.

On the guitar, the 12th fret is exactly halfway between the nut and the bridge, so it will be the location of our first open string harmonics. Touch the string right above the 12th fret—not above the fret space, but above the metal fret itself—and pick. Natural harmonics are also sometimes called "bell," "chime," or "harp" harmonics because of their tone. Here, they are indicated by placing the fret number in a diamond with an "N".

> TIP: Don't press the string down, just touch it lightly, right above the metal fret. After you sound the harmonic, lift off of the string.

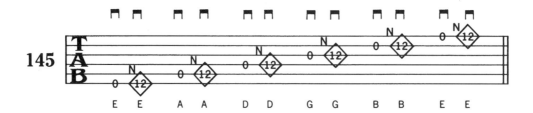

When the string is divided into three equal parts, it vibrates like this:

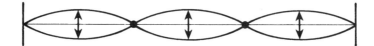

This second harmonic may be produced by touching the string at either of the nodes, which occur at the 7th and 19th frets. The pitch is an octave and a fifth (that's five tones of the major scale) above the open string. Or you can think of it as being just one octave above the fretted note at the 7th fret.

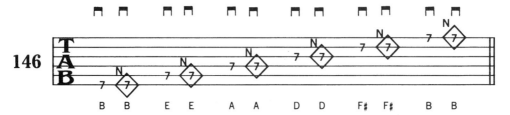

Dividing a string into four equal parts raises the pitch two octaves above the open string. You can find this harmonic at either the 5th or 24th frets.

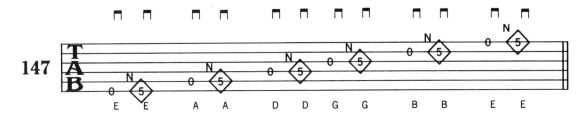

Dividing a string into five equal parts raises the pitch two octaves plus a major third (three tones of the major scale) above the open string. Or you can think of this harmonic as being two octaves above the fretted note at the 4th fret.

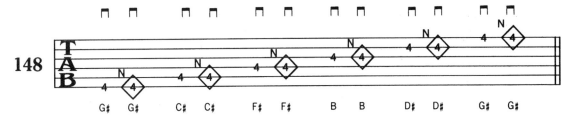

Dividing a string into six equal parts raises the pitch two octaves plus a fifth above the open string. This occurs just slightly higher than the 3rd fret. The harmonic series continues but the harmonics become more and more difficult to produce as the vibration lengths get shorter.

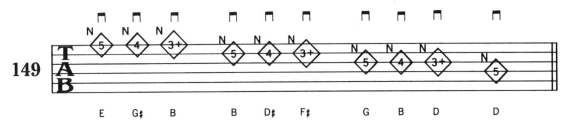

Example 150 is a short rhythm riff with a lead fill that is comprised of natural harmonics.

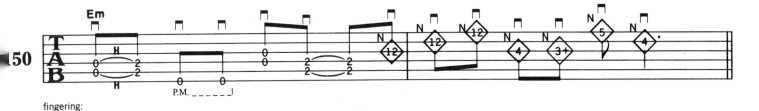

fingering:

THE VIBRATO BAR ◆44◆

The vibrato bar, also called the tremolo arm, whammy bar, or wang bar, as well as a few other less dignified terms, has become almost standard equipment in metal guitar. Here, we'll cover just a few things you can do with it. Of course if you don't have a vibrato bar on your guitar, you'll have to sit this one out.

The first effect is called simply "dipping" the bar. This is done by slightly and quickly depressing and releasing the bar. Listen the example 151 and copy the sound.

Another common effect is diving, or "divebombing." In the example below, first the G string is picked. Let it ring for a second, then drop the bar down slowly to dive.

Diving with the bar is particularly attention-getting with high pitched harmonics.

For better sustain, try pulling off to the open string as extra hard instead of picking. But be careful to keep the unwanted strings from ringing also. In example 154, after the first dive on the low E string, pull off onto the fifth string and come back up to pitch, for this Eddie Van Halen-style technique.

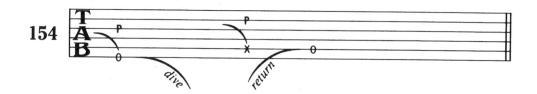

In example 155, practice releasing the bar immediately after the dive, to sound the chord.

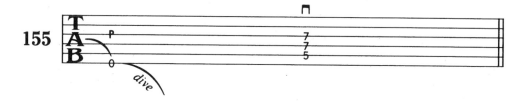

In example 156, slowly dive with the bar while playing the hammers and pulls with the left hand. Notice that the first note is sounded without a previous note ringing—a hammer-on from "nowhere."

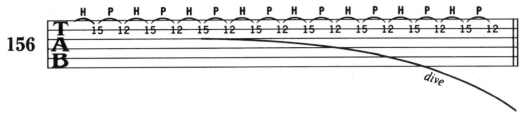

For example 157, do the same but shake the bar up and down.

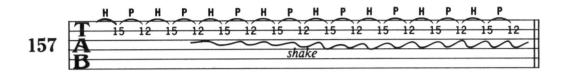

Next is another technique that involves dipping, or lightly tapping, the bar. Hammer on the first note as lightly dip the bar. Then the following two notes are played with a hammer and pull. Tap the bar again and repeat, etc.

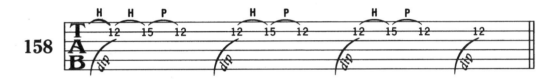

This time dip the bar with each note.

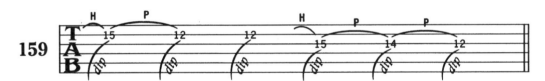

Vibrato can also be put on natural harmonics using the vibrato bar. Listen to example 160 and copy the sound.

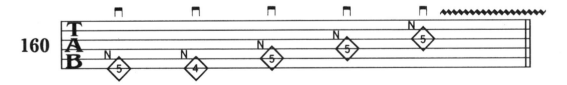

Example 161 is a Joe Satriani-style approach. Here's the procedure: Dive on the open G string. Then lightly touch the 5th fret natural harmonic and release the bar back up. If you have a floating vibrato system, keep pulling right on past the original position as high as it will go. Then dive again. (If you don't have a floating vibrato, just dive after the harmonic hits its normal pitch.)

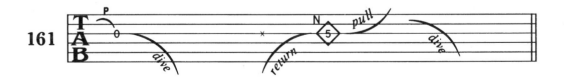

This is by no means the limit of what you can do with the bar—its just the beginning. Experiment with these tricks and see what else you can come up with! You can also check out Metal Guitar Tricks for more ideas.

RIGHT-HANDED FRETTING ◆45

Popularized by Eddie Van Halen, first in his groundbreaking "Eruption" solo as well as many others that followed, right-handed fretting or tapping has become a staple of metal lead guitar. Once considered a special "trick," it is now solidly in place as a part of the metal guitar repertoire, and simply regarded as an alternative playing approach which opens up the fretboard to a whole new set of possibilities. Today, players such as Joe Satriani continue to refine and expand its applications.

Below, the basic tapping pattern used by Eddie Van Halen in his "Eruption" solo (and others) is shown. Hammer-on with either the index or middle finger of the right hand to sound the first note of the triplet. Pull it off to sound the second note, and then hammer with your third finger to play the third note. Take care to keep the other strings quiet as best you can.

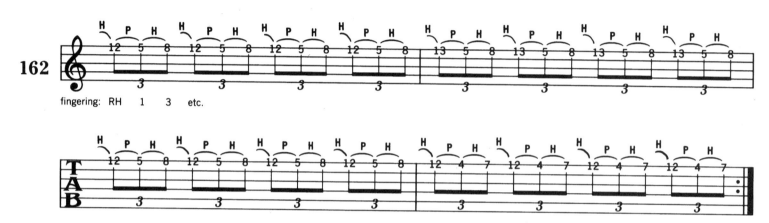

The next two licks use groups of four notes, with different combinations of hammers and pulls in the left hand. Still, the right hand marks the beginning of each note group.

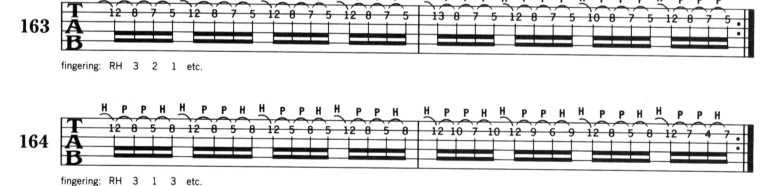

In the next example, sweep up the string with your right-hand first finger after you tap. Then, after you slide up the neck, pull it off to sound the next note.

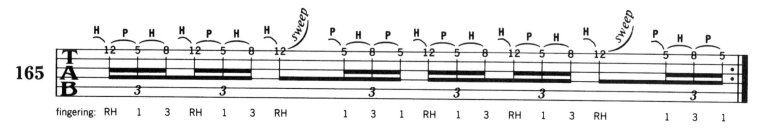

Another common right hand "Van Halenism" combines bending with right hand fretting. Below, the string is bent up a whole step, then the right hand hammers down to fret on that bent string. Since the string remains bent, the pitch will sound two frets higher than the note which is fretted by the right hand. Use your left hand to produce a vibrato bend.

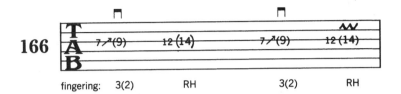

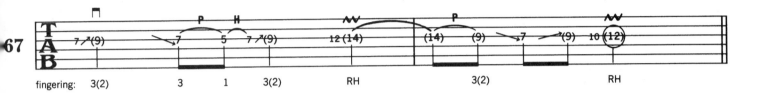

SPEED EXERCISES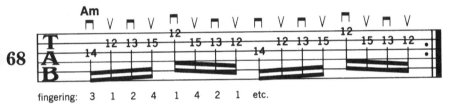

Hey, you know the drill. Crank it up!

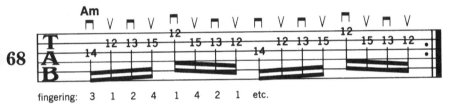

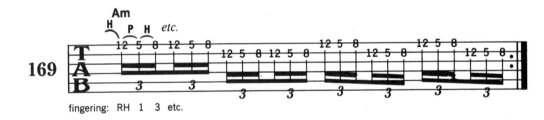

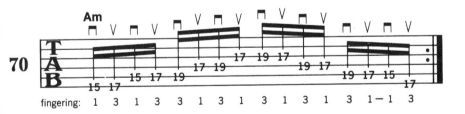

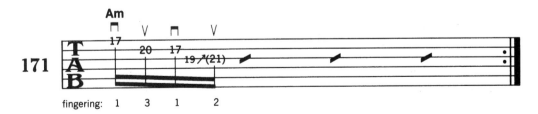

"Into the Spotlight" features a faster tempo with typical metal pedal-tone riffs and progressions in the key of A minor. Again, the form is ABABA, with B representing solo sections. The solo itself blends together some dangerous alternate picking runs, hammer/pull licks, natural harmonics, the vibrato bar, and of course, some right hand fretting. Practice each phrase to get it up to speed, then practice switching between the normal playing position and the right handed fretting positions. You want to be able to make the change seamlessly.

INTO THE SPOTLIGHT 🔷47
(Solo #6)

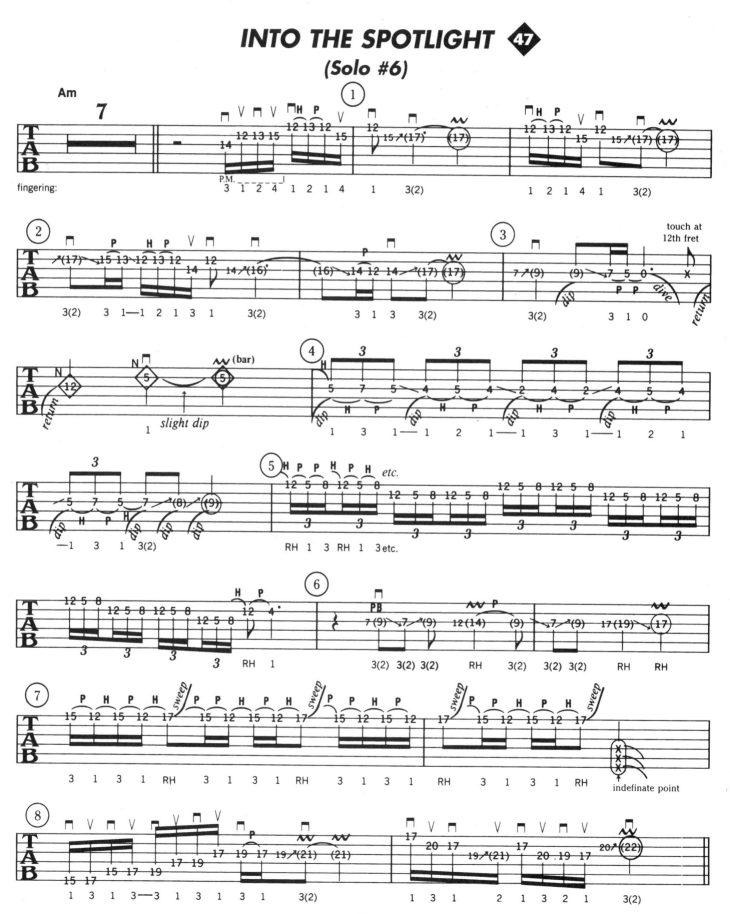

**Congratulations!
You've made it to the end of Volume 1!**

Here is just some of what is waiting for you in Volume 2—

·

The modes and how to use them,

more exotic scales such as phrygian-dominant,

chromatic, and harmonic minor,

more phrasing and rhythmic concepts,

more speed exercises,

music theory of keys, scale structures and their interrelationships,

how to solo in major keys,

arpeggios and how to emphasize underlying chord progressions,

how to determine which scales will work over chord progressions,

intervals and harmony,

chord resolution,

intro to sweep picking,

extended scale patterns to complete the neck, and

right-handed tapping for arpeggiated chord progressions.

·

143 more licks and examples,

five more full solos with backing tracks,

plus

the complete lead track to the instrumental, Babylon.

KEEPING TABS ON YOUR OWN KILLER LICKS

Use the blank tabs on the following pages to write out some of your own hottest licks, and create variations on them. Be bold! And try using them in your improvisations. When you've filled up these tabs, get a book of blank tab-staff manuscript paper and keep going. This is a very helpful step in developing your own lead style.

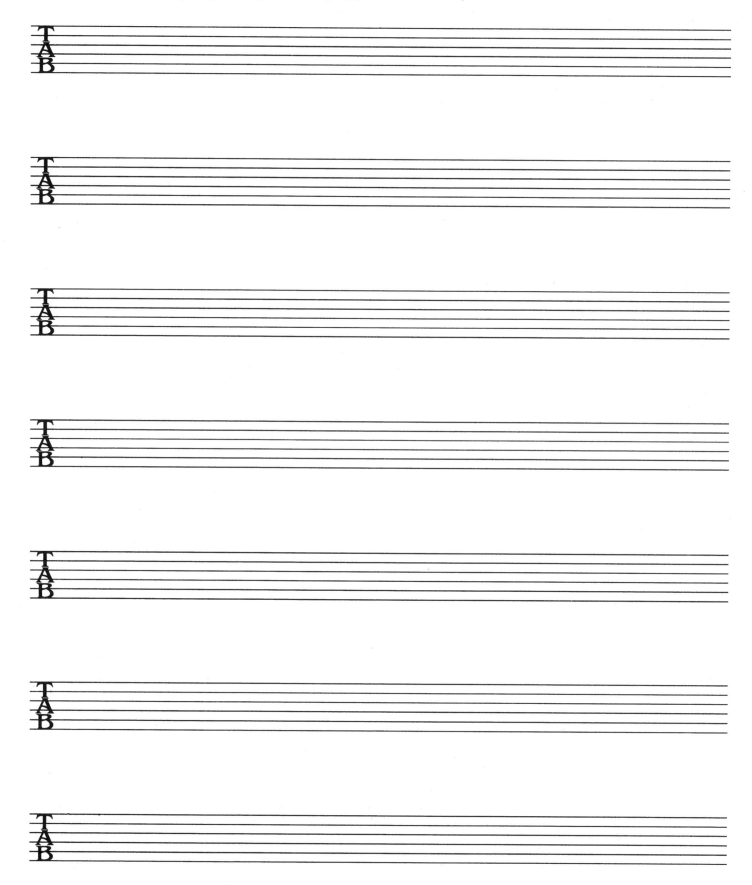

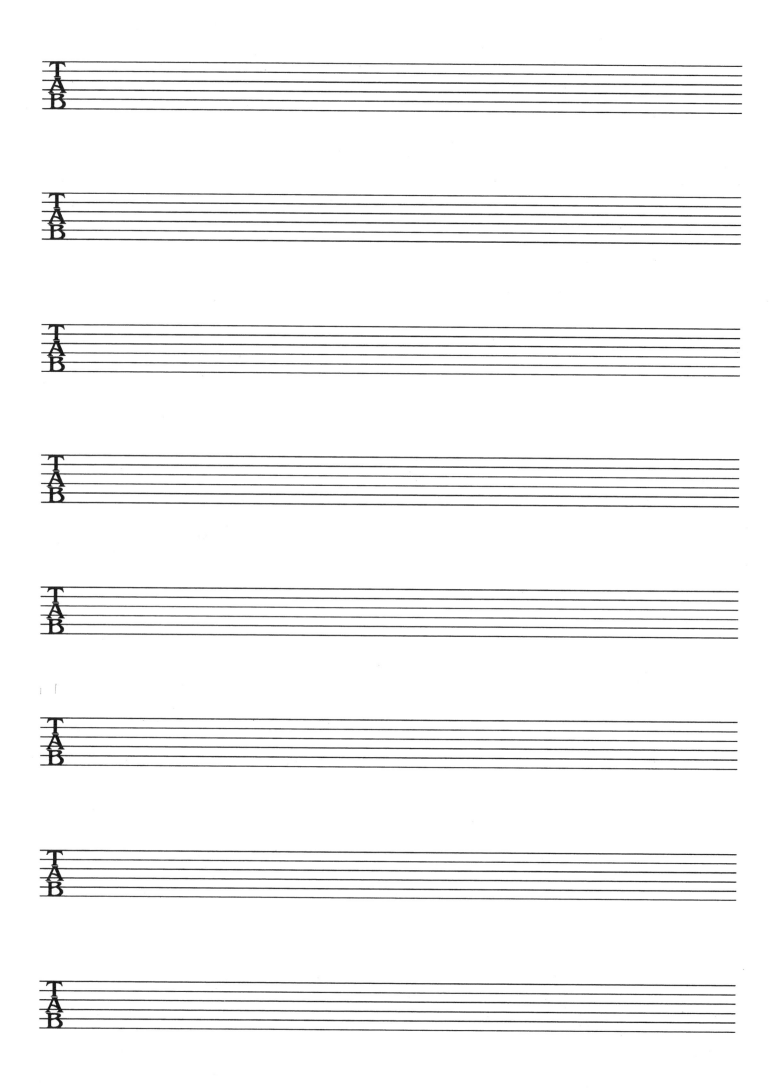

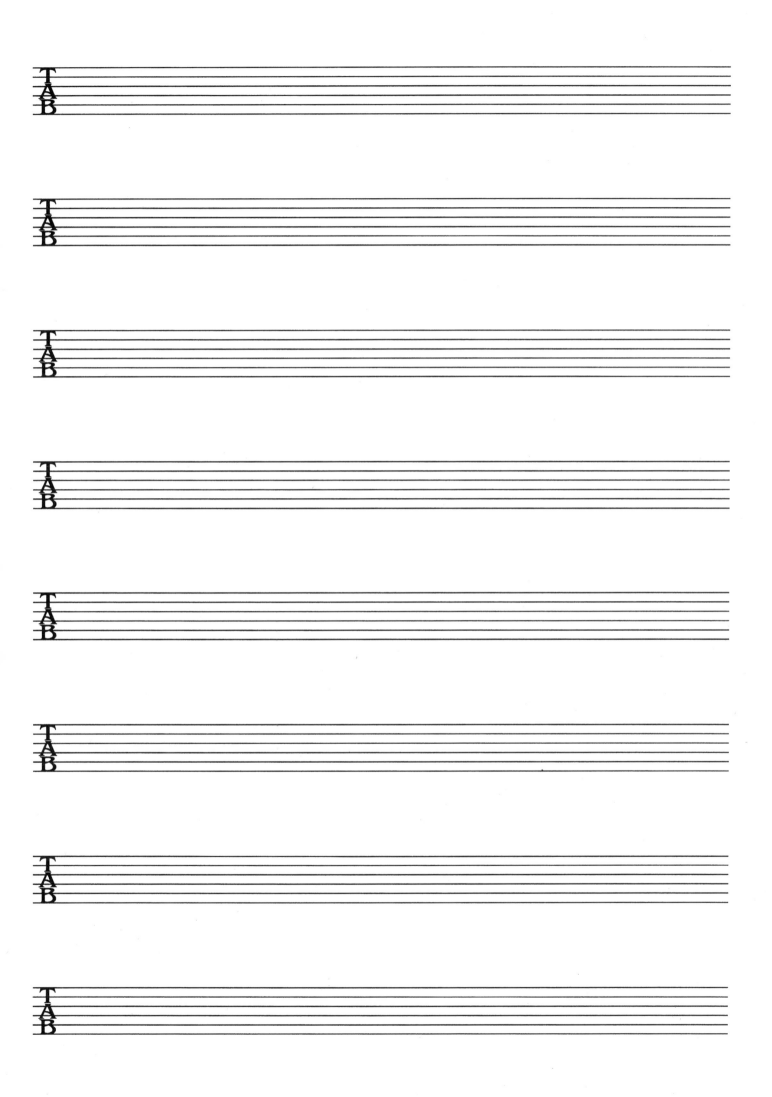

NOTATION GUIDE

Whole Note   Half Note   Quarter Note   Eigth Notes   Sixteeth Notes

Bend at 15th fret- (whole step) Target pitch in parenthesis   Immediate Bend (or, grace note bend)   Bend & Release   Bend (half step)   Bend (Step and a half)   Pre-bend and release

Vibrato   Vibrato bend   Picking indications (Downstroke & upstroke)   Rake strings   Left hand mute (Percussive tone -no pitch)   Palm-mute

Staccato phrasing   Hammer-on technique   Pull-off technique   Slide   Slide up to note from indeterminate point   Slide down from note

Vibrato bar dipping   Vibrato bar diving, or scooping   Right hand tapping   Bend & tap technique

Slide up to indeterminate point & back down neck   Pick Scrape   Artificial harmonics (Also, pinch or pick harmonics)   Natural Harmonics   Tap harmonics

GLOSSARY OF TERMS

Scale. A particular set of notes beginning on one pitch, called the root, and continuing up to the octave of that root note. A seven tone scale is called a *diatonic* scale, and a five tone scale is a *pentatonic* scale. Also, *relative* scales are scales that share the same notes, but use different roots. *Parallel* scales share the same root, but use different notes.

Mode. A type of scale created by displacing the root of another scale. Modes can be created from any scale.

Tone. As used in this method, *tone* refers to the numbered relationship of a pitch to the root note of the scale. For example 1, 2, ♭3, or root, second, minor third are *tones*.

Note. A certain pitch, generally specified by a letter name. For example, A, C, F♯.

Rhythm. Generally, the whole timing aspect and length of notes. Also can refer to a specific sequence of timing values. For example, a *rhythm* of eighth notes.

Beat. The underlying pulse in music, in relation to which, the length and timing of notes is measured.

Riff. A short, self-contained musical thought, or phrase which appears repeatedly and plays an important role in a song. Tends to be specific to rock and metal.

Lick. Refers to rock and metal lead guitar phrases that generally involve string bending or other guitar techniques. A loosely defined term, licks are also sometimes called riffs.

Chord. More than one note sounding together at the same time.

Arpeggio. The notes of a chord played one after another, in sequence.

Harmony. Two or more notes sounding together. Usually refers to a *secondary melody* which supports and strengthens the main melody.

Interval. The distance between two notes. The steps of the major scale are used to name intervals, as in a *major third* or *perfect fifth*. Also, a *whole step* is an interval of two frets, a *half step* is an interval of one fret.

Chromatic. Using every half step, as opposed to diatonic, which would follow the steps of the major or minor scale.

Form. Refers to the overall, or large scale structure of music. Letters, starting with A, B, C, etc., are used as variables to denote different sections of music. For example, form AABA is known as the basic song form, with A standing for a verse/chorus section and B standing for a bridge/solo section.

More Great Titles from
TROY STETINA

FRETBOARD MASTERY
INCLUDES TAB

Familiarizes you with all the shapes you need to know by applying them in real musical examples, thereby reinforcing and reaffirming your newfound knowledge.

00695331 Book/Online Audio.........................$19.95

METAL LEAD GUITAR PRIMER

earn metal guitar the best way - by playing music! This primer for the beginning lead guitarist builds the solid musical and technical foundation you'll need as it prepares you for Metal Lead Guitar Vol. 1 with several metal 'jams'. Whether trading licks with the pre-recorded leads, or soloing by yourself, these rhythm tracks with full band accompaniment will make you sound great and they're fun to play! A great starter book – no experience necessary! Includes tablature. 48-minute audio accompaniment.

00660316 Book/Online Audio.........................$19.99

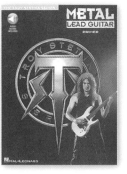

METAL LEAD GUITAR

This intense metal method teaches you the elements of lead guitar technique with an easy to understand, player-oriented approach. The metal concepts, theory, and musical principles are all applied to real metal licks, runs and full compositions. Learn at your own pace through 12 fully transcribed heavy metal solos from simple to truly terrifying! Music and examples demonstrated on the online audio. "One of the most thorough" and "one of the best rock series currently available" – *Guitar Player* magazine.

00699321 Volume 1 – Book/Online Audio....................$19.99
00699322 Volume 2 – Book/Online Audio....................$19.99

METAL RHYTHM GUITAR

Because rhythm and timing lie at the foundation of everything you play, its importance can't be underestimated. This series will give you that solid foundation you need. Starts with simple upbeat rhythms for the beginner and moves step by step into advanced syncopations – all demonstrated with seriously heavy metal examples that have practical applications to today's styles. Tablature. Music and examples demonstrated on the online audio.

00699319 Volume 1 – Book/Online Audio....................$19.99
00699320 Volume 2 – Book/Online Audio....................$19.99

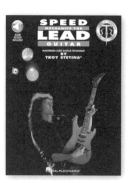

SPEED MECHANICS FOR LEAD GUITAR
INCLUDES TAB

Learn the fastest ways to achieve speed and control, secrets to make your practice time really count, and how to open your ears and make your musical ideas more solid and tangible. Packed with over 200 vicious exercises. 89-minute audio.

00699323 Book/Online Audio.........................$19.99

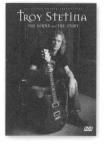

TROY STETINA – THE SOUND AND THE STORY
DVD

ALL-ACCESS GUITAR INSTRUCTION
Fret12

Topics covered include: the path to unlimited speed, control and articulation • ultimate shred picking secrets • non-standard phrasing ideas and bending approaches • secrets to playing in the pocket and building engaging riffs • arrangement tips and compositional ideas • and more. Approximately 3 hrs., 30 min.

00321271 DVD...$28.95

THRASH GUITAR METHOD

by Troy Stetina and Tony Burton

Let the mosh begin! This truly radical method book takes you from slow grinding metal up to the fastest thrashing. Syncopation, shifting accents, thrash theory, progressions, chromatic 'ear-twisting' melodic dissonances, shifting time signatures, harmony, and more. The online audio features bull band accompaniment for all musical examples so that you can play along with the band. Fully transcribed in tablature!

00697218 Book/Online Audio.........................$19.99

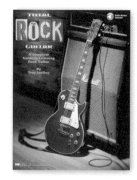

TOTAL ROCK GUITAR
INCLUDES TAB

A COMPLETE GUIDE TO LEARNING ROCK GUITAR

Total Rock Guitar is a unique and comprehensive source for learning rock guitar, designed to develop both lead and rhythm playing. This book covers: getting a tone that rocks; open chords, power chords and barre chords; riffs, scales and licks; string bending, strumming, palm muting, harmonics and alternate picking; all rock styles; and much more. The examples in the book are in standard notation with chord grids and tablature, and the online audio includes full-band backing for all 22 songs.

00695246 Book/Online Audio.........................$19.99

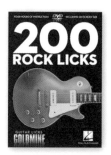

200 ROCK LICKS
DVD INCLUDES TAB

GUITAR LICKS GOLDMINE

featuring Greg Harrison, Matthew Schroeder and Troy Stetina

A *Guitar Licks Goldmine* awaits in this incredible rock collection! This DVD is jam-packed with killer lead lines, phrases, and riffs personally taught to you by professional guitarists Greg Harrison, Matthew Schroeder, and Troy Stetina. From classic rock to modern metal, each and every authentic lick includes: a walk-through explanation by a pro guitarist; note-for-note on-screen tablature; normal and slow-speed performance demos. 4 hours, 14 minutes.

00320930 DVD...$24.99

HAL·LEONARD®
www.halleonard.com